Overdoing Democracy

Overdoing Democracy

Why We Must Put Politics in its Place

ROBERT B. TALISSE

OXFORD

UNIVERSITY PRESS

OXFORD
UNIVERSITY PRESS

Oxford University Press is a department of the University of Oxford. It furthers
the University's objective of excellence in research, scholarship, and education
by publishing worldwide. Oxford is a registered trade mark of Oxford University
Press in the UK and certain other countries.

Published in the United States of America by Oxford University Press
198 Madison Avenue, New York, NY 10016, United States of America.

Library of Congress Cataloging-in-Publication Data
Names: Talisse, Robert B., author.
Title: Overdoing democracy : why we must put politics in its place /
Robert B. Talisse.
Description: New York, NY : Oxford University Press, [2019] |
Includes bibliographical references and index.
Identifiers: LCCN 2019006875 (print) | LCCN 2019011831 (ebook) |
ISBN 9780190924201 (online content) | ISBN 9780190924218 (updf) |
ISBN 9780190924225 (epub) | ISBN 9780190924195 (cloth : alk. paper) |
ISBN 9780197619100 (paperback)
Subjects: LCSH: Democracy—Philosophy. | Political participation.
Classification: LCC JC423 (ebook) | LCC JC423 .T2746 2019 (print) |
DDC 321.8—dc23
LC record available at https://lccn.loc.gov/2019006875

1 3 5 7 9 8 6 4 2

Printed by LSC Communications, United States of America

Contents

III. PRESCRIPTION

Foreword to the Paperback Edition

Overdoing Democracy emerged out of the ordeal of the 2016 US Presidential election. Readers will recall that the months leading up to Election Day were especially rancorous. Every day brought a new alleged scandal, gaffe, or outrage. The two major candidates, Hillary Clinton and Donald Trump, were both in full combat mode, each declaring the other fundamentally unfit for public office. Trump went farther, declaring Clinton a criminal. During an October debate, Trump claimed that were he elected, he'd put Clinton in jail. It was an ugly chapter in US electoral politics.

As the contest for the Presidency grew more acrimonious, public discussion about the election became inescapable. A trip to the grocery store or gas station could easily turn into a political summit among strangers: "Can you believe what Hillary did?" or "Did you hear Trump last night?" The ensuing conversations often focused mainly on the demeanor and character of the candidates, frequently escalating into expressions of indignation and outrage. Only rarely were the candidates' official platforms and policy commitments mentioned. And even when they were, discussion rarely went beyond the candidates' campaign slogans and attack lines.

I found it exhausting. So, I conducted an informal experiment. Whenever someone would strike up a conversation by saying things like, "Did you see that Trump tape?" or "Did you hear what Hillary called Republicans?," I would respond by saying "Yes, but I haven't decided yet what to think about it." I expected this response would be a polite signal that I had no interest in a political discussion. Still, I wasn't sure how would-be interlocutors might react.

As it turned out, my response was almost always taken as a request for more information. After saying, "I'm not sure what to think about that," I typically would be briefed on the incident in question. As one might expect, although my interlocutor would present the report as a simple retelling of the facts, it would almost always conclude with a *judgment* with which I was expected instantly to agree: "She's horrible," or "What a creep." In response to the summary verdict, I would offer a second response like my first: "Well, maybe—but I'm still thinking about it."

I had guessed that this second reply would be received as a polite end to the discussion. Yet most interactions continued. My second "I'm still thinking" response was commonly taken as an expression of doubt about whether the campaign news had been accurately conveyed: "No—she *literally* said Republicans are deplorable." In many of these instances, my uncommitting response was understood to be an affront, as if I had expressed an opposing verdict. This led some interlocutors to escalate.

In one memorable exchange about Hillary Clinton's "deplorables" remark, a person told me, "Well, she's an elitist, and I see that you probably are too." Here, my expression of indecision about Hillary's comment was interpreted as *approval* of what she had said. On a different occasion, an interlocutor expressed relief that Clinton had "finally called the Republicans what they are." Cautiously, I responded that Hillary's comment was not directed at Republicans as such but only at certain Trump supporters. To this my interlocutor said, "But these people *really are* deplorable; if you won't acknowledge that, I'm wasting my time talking to you."

I was involved in more than a dozen interactions that fit these general patterns. My initial expression of indecision was taken as revealing that I lacked information. And once the interlocutor filled me in, it was assumed that I would be positioned to render a verdict. In other words, my interlocutors assumed that knowing what to think was *simply* a matter of having the facts. The idea that campaign slipups, and even offenses, might call for reflection seemed to have been abandoned. It seemed not to have occurred to my interlocutors that sometimes the important thing about gaffes and missteps is *how the candidate reacts* to being criticized for them. Although these interactions were introduced as occasions for political deliberation, they were more like micro-targeted small-scale campaign events. Partisan evaluation was expected to be instantaneous, and even indecision was interpreted as a firm expression of party allegiance.

It occurred to me that these encounters reflected broader social trends: In the United States and other democracies, day-to-day life has become increasingly organized around the categories and fissures of our politics. For a long time, I saw this as a sign of democratic health. I had figured that the interweaving of partisan identities with our day-to-day activities was a byproduct of people taking citizenship seriously. We should expect politics to saturate our social lives. Democracy is a full-time job, after all.

Yet in 2016, something seemed amiss. It wasn't simply that the election had turned uncommonly nasty. It felt as if democratic politics in the United States had changed. Our partisan divides were being cast not as differences about good or bad government, but as fundamentally *existential*—a conflict over democracy itself, and thus the survival of the nation. A diagnosis was needed.

I got to thinking that our social lives are *bounded* such that the centering of certain kinds of collective goods can *expel* or crowd out others. But that's not all. In some cases, the expelled goods can be central to the value of the centered goods. In other words, it is possible to *undermine* or *spoil* a good by pursuing it *in the absence of* the pursuit of certain other goods. This is because some goods have as part of their profile the enabling or furthering of others. When goods of this kind are pursued to the exclusion of all else, their value is therefore diminished.

This led to the idea that the collective goods of democracy could be spoiled by their singular, constant enactment and pursuit. Conjoining this with views I had about the political implications of the cognitive phenomenon called *belief* polarization encouraged a further idea: The *extent* to which politics had saturated social space could be democratically dysfunctional. In exercising democratic citizenship under conditions of political saturation, we could erode our democratic capacities, the attitudes and dispositions we need in order to perform well as citizens. It struck me that it is possible to *overdo* democracy.

As I emphasize throughout this book, it's important to state things carefully. The idea that it's possible to overdo democracy is *not* the claim that we need to disengage or withdraw from politics, leaving governing to elites or experts. Nor is it the idea that we need to learn reconcile with our political enemies, set our differences aside, and reach for consensus. Disengagement is not a *democratic* option. And reconciliation is often not really an *option* among democratic citizens.

Overdoing Democracy embraces the premise that in a democracy, we need to do politics together. We need to be active participants in the joint project of self-government among political equals. This means that democracy will involve significant disagreements, disputes in which opponents see one another as not only wrong, but *in the wrong*. Such disputes are naturally volatile, heated, and acrimonious. There is no mode of democratic politics that can insulate citizens from the rancor and hostility of partisan opposition. The task for democracy is to *manage* political conflict, not evade it.

Centrally, the task of managing political conflict within a democracy is that of sustaining among citizens the capacity to regard their political opponents as nonetheless political equals. I call this democratic relation among citizens *civic friendship*, and I devote Chapter Five to spelling out what it requires. The point is that when politics structures *everything* we do together, we heighten our exposure to belief polarization. This leads us to regard one another as *defined* by partisan loyalties. We see our fellow citizens *strictly* as allies or enemies. We come to regard our partisan opponents as threats to the democratic enterprise as such. Civic friendship dissolves, all as a consequence of enthusiastic political engagement.

That last point is crucial. Overdoing democracy results from activities that are otherwise commendable. This is why the problem of overdoing democracy cannot be addressed by democracy itself. It turns out that Jane Addams and John Dewey were mistaken in saying that the cure for democracy's ills is more and better democracy. Overdoing democracy is one political dysfunction that democracy itself can't remedy. Democracy is subject to a kind of auto-immune disorder.

The prescription, then, follows directly from the diagnosis. Democratic citizens need to claim regions of social space for nonpolitical cooperative endeavors. They need, occasionally, to do things together in which politics is not suppressed, but simply beside the point.

Again, it's crucial to express things carefully. The idea is *not* that we must make friends of our partisan enemies, invite them over for coffee, or play softball with them. We *may* do these things, of course. But initiatives of this kind keep politics firmly at the center of the undertaking. We "reach across the aisle" or join a bi-partisan bowling team *as an act of partisanship*, a way of affirming the broad-mindedness of our political coalition. The prescription rather is to engage in cooperative activities where we simply don't know one another's politics, not because we have mutually agreed to suppress them, but because the point of the enterprise lies elsewhere. The hope is that, by engaging in such activities, we can view one another's virtues in contexts that do not tie them specifically to our favored partisan identities. We try to see one another as responsible, caring, conscientious, and thoughtful *outside of* politics so that when we come to engage politically, we will be less inclined to dismiss our opponents as failed human beings. We can see them instead simply as wrong about politics.

I realize that the very idea of a nonpolitical cooperative endeavor strains the imagination. Critics often point to that strain as evidence that the prescription of *Overdoing Democracy* is a nonstarter or perhaps incoherent. As I see it, the difficulty we have in imagining a cooperative endeavor that's nonetheless not an expression of our politics is rather a *symptom* of overdoing democracy. We have grown so accustomed to the idea that everything we do together must be an enactment of our partisan identities that we can no longer even *conceive* of a mode of nonpolitical pro-social interaction. But, if the argument of *Overdoing Democracy* is sound, this condition is democratically debilitating.

I write this new Foreword in the wake of the 2020 US Presidential Election. The months following Election Day have been remarkable, to put it mildly. Unsubstantiated charges of widespread voter fraud and electoral malfeasance, promoted by Donald Trump and others, led to an insurrectionist riot at the US Capitol on January 6, an attempt to stop the US Congress from certifying Joe Biden's victory. The dysfunctional trends outlined in this book have become all the more manifest.

In his Inaugural Address, President Biden understandably called for unity, that "most elusive" thing in our democracy. Unity is necessary, Biden said, to defeat our "common foes" like "anger, resentment, hatred," "extremism, lawlessness, violence," and "disease, joblessness, hopelessness." Biden's overriding message was clear: in the prior four years, our democratic politics had gone off the rails. The country needs to get back on track.

It makes for inspiring rhetoric, but ultimately, the call for unity keeps politics at the center. For this reason, the exhortation provides a new site for the same partisan divisions. To see this, note that Biden's call for unity is vacuous unless he specifies *something around which* to unify. Unity must have an object, so to speak. But once the object of our envisioned unity is identified, Biden's opponents see it as a brute projection of his political agenda. Those who reject Biden's politics hear the call for unity as a demand for capitulation. Why should they unify around the other party's priorities? Once defined, unity is divisive.

This might be why Biden left the term vague. But this strategy raises a difficulty of its own. In calling for an indefinite unity,

Biden invites opponents to supply their own definition of the term. Republicans hence swiftly charged Biden with sowing division and betraying unity, simply in virtue of pursuing the policy and legislative agenda upon which he campaigned. As interpreted by his partisan opponents, unity requires Biden to govern in a way that provokes no objection from Republicans. The dominant view among his opposition is that in order to serve unity, Biden must govern like a Republican.

Unity thus raises a paradox. In urging the nation to unify, Biden must either specify what he means by "unity," or leave the term vague. Either way, the call for unity incites our divisions. Exhortations to unity are self-defeating.

To be clear, Biden is correct that the country needs to restore the democratic common ground. We must reaffirm our commitment to the idea that, despite our divisions, we remain equal partners in the joint task of perfecting our democratic republic. Sharing that reaffirmation is a kind of unity.

But unity in that sense is elusive precisely because, like other important interpersonal goods such as friendship or love, it cannot be summoned, demanded, or exhorted. To pick up on a point made throughout *Overdoing Democracy*, we realize goods like these only by striving together for other things. Friendship, for example, forms among people who join together for purposes *other than* making friends. Treating "making friends" as the objective of an interaction is surely the worst way to go about making friends. Similarly, striving for unity can't bring us together. It only entrenches our divisions.

We thus return to the idea that there are democratic dysfunctions that cannot be addressed by democracy itself. It turns out that democracy's flourishing depends on there being healthy interpersonal relations among persons beyond their political roles. In the absence of relations of that broader kind, citizenship erodes, and democracy suffers.

Importantly, the argument of *Overdoing Democracy* is not driven by the premise that we must devote our lives to making democracy work. My broader point has to do with the place of democratic politics in our efforts to lead valuable lives. In a nutshell, the argument shows that if we allow democracy to colonize the entirety of our social worlds, we impoverish our lives. We crowd out those goods and pursuits that cannot be cast as contributions to our political objectives; we lose out on enriching experiences and relationships that lie beyond politics. That's worse than political dysfunction. It's a kind of moral tragedy.

After all, part of what makes democracy so precious is that it promises a relatively just, stable, and decent social order that allows people to devote their lives to other things besides citizenship— modes of attachment, care, love, creativity, and devotion that are larger than politics. Although democracy may be necessary to live well, we simply cannot live well by politics alone.

March 2021, Nashville, TN

Acknowledgments

The irony is not lost on me. This book is about the need to attend to things other than democratic politics, and yet my entire career as a professional philosopher has been devoted to thinking about democracy. Perhaps it is fitting, then, that I begin by thanking friends and family, most of whom are not academics, who have provided rich outlets for social engagement that are rarely focused on politics. First among these is my wife, Joanne Billett, who remains a source of deep insight, sound advice, new ideas, and, most importantly, attachments to things whose value I otherwise would have overlooked. My mother, Patricia Talisse, supplies support simply by means of her enthusiasm for (almost) anything I do. In the course of writing this book, I've been benefitted in a similar way by regular discussions and visits with long-time non-philosopher friends with whom I share histories stretching back to the time before I took up an academic career: Theano Apostolou, Donna Baker, Michael Calamari, Matt Cotter, Julie Hwang, Dave McCullough, and Edward Taylor.

Of course, colleagues can also be friends. There is much in this book that has been improved as a result of my friendship and ongoing philosophical collaboration with Scott Aikin. Scott not only read most of the manuscript, he also welcomed scores of impromptu discussions about the ideas it contains. No doubt several of these conversations began as a sudden interruption of his own work, so I am appreciative of his forbearance. In any case, Scott helped me think through many of the details of the view I present here. More importantly, he also provided occasions for thinking philosophically about things *other than* democratic politics. Another colleague and friend, Jeffrey Tlumak, provided a similar kind of assistance. As anyone who knows him will attest, Jeffrey is the most generous and thoughtful interlocutor one could hope to encounter. Jeffrey also tolerated regular intrusions into his office to ask for advice, guidance, or an intuition-check.

Now for more traditional acknowledgments. The following friends, colleagues, teachers, and students are to be thanked for helping me in writing this book, either by commenting on draft chapters, responding to emailed queries, sharing related work of their own, pressing criticisms and objections at conferences, or simply asking questions in the course of casual discussion: Kristof Ahlstrom-Vij, Elizabeth Anderson, Jody Azzouni, Michael Bacon, Elizabeth Barone, William James Booth, Jonathan Bremer, Thom Brooks, Kimberley Brownlee, F. Thomas Burke, Mary Butterfield, Ann Cacoullos, Steven Cahn, Gregg Caruso, John Casey, Tom Christiano, Caleb Clanton, Matt Congdon, Wout Cornelissen, John Corvino, Rebecca Davenport, Jeroen de Ridder, Idit Dobbs-Weinstein, Catarina Dutilh Novaes, Maureen Eckert, Elizabeth Edenberg, David Edmonds, David Estlund, Carrie Figdor, Elizabeth Fiss, Andrew Forcehimes, Shannon Fyfe, Jerry Gaus, Eddie Glaude, Sandy Goldberg, Lenn Goodman, David Miguel Gray, Alex Guerrero, Hanna Gunn, Michael Hannon, Nicole Hassoun, Michael Harbour, Fiacha Heneghan, Diana Heney, D. Micah Hester, David Hildebrand, Michael Hodges, Shanto Iyengar, Gary Jaeger, Angelo Juffras, Klemens Kappel, David Kaspar, John Lachs, Helene Landemore, Anabelle Lever, Tania Levey, Alyssa Lowery, Michael Lynch, Kate Manne, Michele Margolis, Mason Marshall, Takunda Matose, Amy McKiernan, Darla Migan, Sarah Clark Miller, Josh Miller, Christian Miller, Cheryl Misak, Jonathan Neufeld, Karen Ng, Brian O'Connor, John O'Connor, Lou Outlaw, John Peterman, Jeanne Palomino, Fabienne Peter, Lyn Radke, Yvonne Raley, Regina Rini, David Rondel, Luke Semrau, Aaron Simmons, Peter Simpson, Karen Stohr, Cass Sunstein, Paul Taylor, Rob Tempio, Lawrence Torcello, Nigel Warburton, Leif Wenar, John Weymark, and Julian Wuerth.

In addition, I thank Lisa Madura for providing exceptional research assistance in addition to good philosophical discussion and sound advice. Once again, Nicole Heller provided expert guidance on matters of grammar and style. I also thank Lucy Randall and Hannah Doyle at Oxford University Press for their guidance and support.

Portions of this book draw from material that was presented at various conferences and other forums. I thank the organizers of the following events and also those who attended them: The Epistemology and Ethics Workshop at Fordham University (September 2016); the Intellectual Humility and Public Deliberation Conference at University of Connecticut (November 2016); the Deliberative Democracy Symposium at University of Canberra (December 2016); the Philosophy Colloquium at University of Nevada, Las Vegas (February 2017); the Philosophy Colloquium at University of Arizona (March 2017); the University of Copenhagen Political Epistemology Workshop (December 2017); the TEDxNashville Conference (March 2018); the Political Epistemology Conference at University of London (May 2018); the Social Epistemology Network Event at University of Oslo (May 2018); the Political Epistemology workshop at Georgetown (October 2018); and the Philosophy Colloquium at Rochester Institute of Technology (November 2018).

Overdoing Democracy

Introduction

Each November, the people of the United States celebrate Thanksgiving. The holiday is meant to commemorate a group meal between Pilgrims and indigenous people that took place in Plymouth, Massachusetts (or possibly Virginia—historians disagree) in 1621. The feast was organized in celebration of an especially plentiful harvest. Of course, as is always the case with social origin stories, the actual history surrounding the nation's settling and founding is far less idyllic than the Thanksgiving mythology depicts. Nonetheless, today the holiday is celebrated with family over a large dinner, traditionally including turkey and pumpkin pie. Thanksgiving is a day when family, including members who are geographically and temporally extended, gathers to spend time and reflect together on the year that is nearly completed. Hence Thanksgiving is the least commercialized of America's national holidays.

Back in November of 2016, a longtime friend who I hadn't seen in a while asked me to lunch so that we could catch up. Our pleasant chatter eventually turned to the upcoming Thanksgiving holiday, and my friend was consumed with dread. In the week prior to our lunch, the country had elected its forty-fifth president after what seemed to be an unusually long and inexcusably acerbic campaign season. For those who supported Hillary Clinton, the loss was especially dispiriting, as many of them harbored sincere reservations about Donald Trump's fitness for the office that he won. On the other side, Trump's supporters evinced a tendency to gloat in ways suggesting that they regarded his victory as a much-deserved slap in the face to the political establishment, a body that apparently they took to include anyone who didn't vote enthusiastically for Trump.[1] My friend was concerned that her family's Thanksgiving dinner would erupt into a bitter clash between politically opposed relatives.

As we spoke, she mentioned a column she had read in the newspaper offering advice on how one might "survive" Thanksgiving dinner amidst political wrangling. Now, despite the holiday's pensive ambitions, Thanksgiving dinner is a notorious site of familial angst. Consequently, early in every November newspapers, magazines, websites, and television programs offer advice on "surviving" the ordeal of Thanksgiving. Going back several years, one can find columns of this kind that cover the usual fare for large gatherings of relatives—bad cooking, boring conversation, prying questions, ill-behaved children, and so on. In recent years, however, the focus has shifted nearly exclusively on strategies for avoiding or navigating *political disagreement* over the dinner table. Unsurprisingly, this more recent trend has intensified in the wake of the 2016 election.

I'm sure you're already well acquainted with the genre. Still, it might be worthwhile to consider a few contributions from the winter of 2018. Writing in the Opinion section of the *New York Times*, Mary Cella offered a comical list of "safe topics" for discussion over holiday dinner; her list included subjects such as sports, the weather, and traffic—that is, only those topics that one might consider raising with strangers.[2] In the Health section of CNN. com, AJ Willingham reports the advice of Danny Post Senning that in dealing with family over the holidays, one must endeavor to not "take the bait"; after all, Willingham claims, it's a mistake to feel that one must engage in political discussion rather than "smile and take one for the team" when goaded by a relative.[3] In the *Globe and Mail*, Debra Soh recommends physically removing oneself from disputatious conversations, or if possible simply skipping contentious holiday gatherings altogether.[4] It is important to notice that columns of this kind frequently cite staying home as the best policy, while also acknowledging, regretfully, that it is not a live option for many.

When one takes due account of the vagaries of family dynamics and the assortment of other stressors that (thanks to the perpetually expanding Christmas season) are in play at Thanksgiving, the uniformity of the advice given in the genre is striking.[5] But so is the messaging. Surely there is something peculiar in the fact that so many of us should reach for strangers' advice for dealing with a once-a-year dinner with family members. This incongruity is punctuated by the fact we are seeking advice from strangers for managing a dinner whose explicit purpose is to bring family together. Democratic politics is tearing us apart.

This book addresses a problem that lies at the intersection of democratic theory and democratic practice. More specifically, it presents a case for changing how we think about democratic politics by examining a problem with how we presently practice democracy. The argument thus begins from the premise that contemporary democracy is, indeed, troubled. The warrant for this premise strikes me as obvious. Moreover, it also strikes me that this premise is widely shared among those who talk and write about contemporary democratic politics. One might go so far as to say that the only thing on which the gamut of political theorists, commentators, pundits, and citizens from across the political spectrum seem to be agreed is that modern democracy has fallen on rough times.

According to some, modern democracy is plagued by distinctive difficulties arising from globalization, including global instability and problems related to economic inequality, nationalism, racism, immigration, refugees, and poverty. Others see the rise of the Internet and social media as the core problem. There are those who claim that the trouble lies in the 24/7 cable news channels, or untrustworthy journalists; others who take the same view with regard to officeholders and party leaders. Some contend that our political dysfunctions arise from the influx of money into politics;

others cite the fact that the most highly mobilized segments of the citizenry tend also to be the most politically ignorant. And some identify the loss of civility among citizens, politicians, pundits, and journalists as the real problem. These different ways of diagnosing democracy's troubles all have their merits, and it is not my aim in this book to settle any rivalry among them as unitary explanations. The point is simply that the discussion that follows presupposes that not all is well with contemporary democracy.

My aim is to identify a dimension of democracy's trouble that has been overlooked, perhaps because it is constantly in view. This has to do with the *ubiquity* of democratic politics, the saturation of social life with activities and projects that are overtly organized around the categories and divisions of current politics—the political saturation of social space, as it will be called in what follows. Political saturation is an unsurprising outcome of popular ways of conceptualizing the ideal of a democratic society. We tend to think that, as the project of collective self-government among equals is both ongoing and highly valuable, in our lives together we must perpetually enact our role as democratic citizens. Consequently, our social lives tend to be dominated by explicitly political projects. And this means, in turn, that our day-to-day social encounters tend to be structured around our political allegiances. In short, we are overdoing democracy. And in overdoing democracy, we dissolve our capacity to do democracy well. Thus the prescriptive upshot of this book: if we want to improve the condition of democratic politics, we need to occasionally do something together other than politics. We have to put politics in its place.

In this way, the democratic ideal must be reconceived to more explicitly recognize its own constraints. It must incorporate the idea that democracy is worth doing well because there are other things worthy of our pursuit that can be pursued best in a well-functioning democracy, but are nonetheless *not* themselves enactments of democratic politics. To put the point somewhat differently, even if one contends that democracy is intrinsically good, it is still the case that part of democracy's value lies in its capacity to enable the realization of other goods, and some of these goods are not political in nature. When the whole of our civic lives is consumed by democratic political projects, these other goods are crowded out, distorted, and smothered. Yet, as I shall argue, among the goods that are crowded out when we overdo democracy are certain nonpolitical social goods that a thriving democracy needs.

Overdoing democracy undermines democracy. I shall take great pains to demonstrate that this central claim is in no way counter-democratic. The idea is not that democracy must be constrained because elites should rule. Nor is the claim that the reach of democratic government must be minimized, that we must opt for a minimal state. Rather, my thesis is that we must reserve spaces within our social environments for collaborative activities and projects in which politics is simply beside the point. We need activities of these kinds if we are to sustain the dispositions and habits that make democracy function properly. In short, putting politics in its place is necessary for a flourishing democracy.

Back now to the holiday dinner table. A Google search for "survive Thanksgiving politics" yields more than forty million hits. Of course, not all of these results links to a unique entry on the theme; moreover, I have not consulted all of the entries that are unique. But in the hundreds of pieces that have appeared in the past three years in major outlets, one suggestion concerning how to survive the holiday is notably absent. No columnist I have read recommends adopting the stance that Thanksgiving dinner is more important than politics. No one has recommended simply saying to one's politically rancorous relatives that political argument is not to be engaged over Thanksgiving, not because it is disruptive or unpleasant, but rather because it is *irrelevant* given the point of the holiday dinner. I have been unable to find in the "surviving Thanksgiving" genre any exploration of the suggestion that in some contexts political disputation isn't merely to be avoided, bracketed, or suppressed, but instead risen above.

We rise above our political differences when we recognize and affirm that there's more to life than the travails of democracy. That there must be more to life than democratic politics is evident from the fact that democracy serves ends beyond itself; democracy is *for* something, so to speak. Part of the explanation of the value of democracy lies in its ability to enable and empower individuals to pursue valuable life projects that are organized around nonpolitical objectives and consequently have some other point. Current modes of democratic practice operate to obscure this fact. They tend to encourage the view that *everything* is politics, that everything we do together is therefore an instance of democracy, and that each individual's paramount social responsibility is to perpetually exercise the office of citizenship. This all-embracing vision of democracy is remarkably common. It will be argued here that it is not only flawed philosophically, but also politically reckless.

To get a sense of why it is reckless, examine the image on the cover of this book. It depicts a recent finding concerning how morally and emotionally charged political messages are circulated on Twitter.[6] The pattern is striking—we intensely exchange political messages calling for outrage, indignation, fervor, and support only among those who share our general political outlook; although these messages are often *about* those from whom we are politically divided, communication across political divides is markedly rare. Perhaps this finding comes as no surprise. Indeed, one might claim that this is precisely what social media platforms are for—sharing, networking, and collaborating among like-minded people. Yet it will be shown in this book that similar patterns of engagement exist across the entirety of social space, even in places we don't expect to find them and cannot easily detect them. What's more, it will be demonstrated that this general pattern of interaction is becoming inescapable, that our political divides have colonized the entirety of our social environment, structuring the whole of day-to-day experience and interpersonal contact. In the process, we are becoming more alien and inscrutable to those who are politically unlike ourselves, and they are becoming to us increasingly un-hinged, erratic, and unintelligible. As social interactions across po-litical divides become less common, we become less capable of such interaction. Hence the comprehensive political segmentation of the populace is eroding the capacities we need in order to properly enact our roles as democratic citizens. Under such conditions, even our best efforts to more authentically instantiate the democratic ideal of engaged self-government are bound to backfire. This is why calls for bipartisanship and cooperation across partisan divides are insufficient, and in a way misguided. More and better politics cannot be the solution to the problem depicted on the cover of this book because *politics is the problem*. If we hope to repair our de-mocracy, we need to find occasions to do more than "reach across the aisle"; we need also to devise cooperative endeavors in which there is no aisle to reach across, activities where politics plays no part at all.

PART I
FRAMING THE THESIS

1

Can Democracy Be Overdone?

Many years ago an undergraduate student at Hunter College whose name I unfortunately cannot recall proposed the most profound definition of philosophy that I've yet encountered. She declared, "Philosophy is going back to square one." This book begins at square one.

The core thesis defended in this book can be stated directly. In the United States, and other Western democracies as well, politics is being overdone, and this is to the detriment of democracy; accordingly, in order to rehabilitate democracy, citizens need to do less rather than more politics. In a nutshell, even in a democracy, we must put politics in its place.

Although the thesis permits this simple articulation, its precise meaning is misconstrued in the absence of careful elaboration. To be more specific, the claim that democratic politics must be put in its place is liable to be heard as expressing some variety of opposition toward democracy. To be sure, to put something in its place is often to demote, humble, or rebuke it. In this way, the claim that we must put politics in its place can be received as the suggestion that we must suppress or discipline it. Hence it should be affirmed that there is a quite different sense of the phrase that is meant throughout this book. In this other sense, to put something in its place is to place it *correctly*, to put it in its right place. In putting politics in its place, then, we aim to put politics in its *proper* place, to correct for a tendency to overdo democracy. As the phrase is meant in this book, the claim that in a democracy politics must be put in its place involves no derogating or reprimanding of democracy.

skepticism about the intrinsic value of democracy, there remains a strong case to be made on democracy's behalf. As an empirical matter, democracy is highly correlated with the production of crucial social goods of other varieties. Thus democracy can be shown to be *instrumentally* valuable. For example, democracies tend to be socially stable. Revolts, revolutions, coups, and assassinations tend to be rare within democratic states, and democratization seems to be a reliable way to insulate societies from the most violent forms of civic unrest. Relatedly, democratic societies tend to be adept at protecting the civil liberties and basic rights of their citizens; and democracies also tend to have comparatively admirable human rights records. In light of this we can say that democracies tend to do well at eschewing the most appalling forms of injustice. Democratic government moreover is highly correlated with the absence of mass starvation. And, last but most certainly not least, democracies tend not to make war against other democracies.

Together, these considerations present a compelling argument for democracy's instrumental value. And the instrumental argument is further strengthened by the fact that the empirical correlations just mentioned are robust enough to encourage the additional claim that democracy is practically necessary for reliably securing the goods of stability, justice, peace, and plenty. Not only does democracy highly correlate with these goods, non-democracy is highly correlated with their absence and violation.

The instrumental case hence can also support the idea that democracy is the most important social good. Note that those who affirm that democracy has intrinsic value needn't deny the instrumentalist case for democracy's value. The intrinsicalist and instrumentalist disagree only about whether democracy is intrinsically valuable; they need not disagree about its instrumental value. The intrinsicalist can fully embrace the idea that democracy is instrumentally valuable to a degree sufficient to render it the best political arrangement. Thus those who claim that democracy is intrinsically valuable and those who claim that its value is instrumental might nonetheless agree that democracy is the capital social good.

But does any reasonable person need to be convinced of the value of democracy? Don't we already know that democracy is a very important, and perhaps supreme, social good? These questions are well placed. After all, in common parlance the term "democracy" is almost uniformly deployed as a term of commendation. When we describe a process, institution, policy, or practice as democratic, we typically thereby express our approval of it. And, similarly, when we call into question the democratic credentials of some state of affairs, we often thereby criticize it. Employing a term familiar to philosophers, one could say then that the term expresses a *thick concept*.

A word expresses a thick concept when, in its standard uses, it describes things as worthy of a particular normative appraisal. Thick concepts perform double-duty as both descriptive and normative. For instance, to characterize an act as *heroic* is partly to describe it as fit for admiration or approval. Notice that we rarely describe a villain's deeds as heroic, even when they unambiguously manifest some hallmark of a heroic act (say, unflinching persistence in the face of serious danger). The same holds for the term *exclusionary*. It characterizes a state of affairs in a way that in part also proposes a negative appraisal. For a tighter grip on the phenomenon, contrast *exclusionary* with *exclusive*; these arguably have roughly the same descriptive content, but differ crucially in the normative assessment they commend.

Anyway, the concept *democracy* is thick. We use the term in part to describe things as morally upright and admirable. Correspondingly, to characterize a state of affairs as undemocratic is to describe it as unfair, illicit, improper, or worse. To be sure, the positive valence of the word "democracy" is relatively recent. One finds in documents surrounding the founding of the United States passages where democracy is compared unfavorably to a form of government called *republican*. The allegation in these contexts is that democracy is rule of the people, and is thus a system by which the majority tyrannizes over the minority. A republic, by contrast, is a polity where the people are ruled, not by men, but by laws. These days, however, we mean by *democracy* what certain 18th-century thinkers called a *constitutional republic* or *representative government*. We now hold that in a democracy, popular rule is constrained by laws specified in a constitution, which apply to all; thus we understand democracy to be consistent with the rule of law. In other words, modern democracy is a form of republican government.

The story of this shift in the meaning of the word is fascinating, but it lies beyond the scope of our present inquiry. As things stand, we simply observe that it is baked into the vernacular that democracy is a capital social good. And this might be appropriate. Maybe democracy is indeed that kind of good. No feature of this book's argument requires one to deny that.

1.2 Too Much of a Good Thing?

So let's stipulate that democracy is, at the very least, an extremely important social good. This allows us to leave open the question of precisely how great a good democracy is. However great a good one might understand democracy to be, there is nonetheless such a thing as having too much democracy, and so it will be possible for a people to overdo it. When democracy is being overdone, we need to do less of it.

These claims will raise red flags among some readers. They will ask: If democracy is, indeed, such an important social good, how could there be too much of it? It is indeed tempting to infer from the claim that democracy is a social good that is prerequisite for the achievement of many other important goods that more democracy is always better, that there could be no way to have too much democracy, and thus no reason ever to do less. Those who draw this inference likewise reason that any call for putting politics in its place must involve the denial that democracy is a good of that caliber.

As attractive as it may be, this inference is flawed. I suspect that its allure is due to the thickness of the concept *democracy*. In order to see the flaw in the inference, then, it will be helpful to step away from democracy for a moment and look to other examples.

In nearly every other context, we readily acknowledge that it is possible to have too much of a good thing. Take cheesecake. However enjoyable those first bites of cheesecake may be, there comes a point at which subsequent bites are no longer satisfying, and might even be positively displeasing. To be sure, cheesecakes are a particular kind of good. Their value derives from their ability to deliver a particular kind of enjoyable sensation to those who consume them. This renders cheesecakes subject to a phenomenon that economists call *diminishing marginal utility*. To wit, keeping everything else constant, with each bite of cheesecake, the value of the subsequent bites diminishes. When one eats too much cheesecake, one undoes its value. Consequently, although cheesecake is good, one can have too much of it. Cheesecake is among those goods that can be enjoyed only in limited doses.

Clearly not all good things are like cheesecakes. And you can rest assured that I am not about to launch into an argument that associates democracy with cheesecake. Certain good things derive their value from something other than the ability to bring gustatory satisfaction. And there are goods that are not subject to the phenomenon of diminishing marginal utility.

But there is another "too much of a good thing" phenomenon, one which plagues goods of these other kinds. Some goods are such that, when they are pursued to a certain degree or in a certain way, they *crowd out* other goods. And sometimes, one's pursuit of a good crowds out other goods that are—either individually or in combination—just as important as the good being pursued. This phenomenon presents a different sense in which a good might be overdone.

For a simple example, imagine Alice. Alice devotes her life to the worthy goal of being physically fit. But suppose also that Alice has adopted the goal of fitness so single-mindedly that the pursuit leaves no time for other good activities that she regards as particularly valuable—socializing with friends and travelling, let's say. It is crucial to notice here that I am not proposing a case in which Alice's pursuit of fitness leads to physical harm, and thereby undermines itself; we need not assume that Alice is overdoing her exercise routine and thus undercutting her fitness. Rather, we are imagining that Alice has adopted the goal of physical fitness in a way that is, we might say, *consuming*. Everything she does is directed toward the goal of improving her physical fitness. The places she frequents, the books she reads, the food she eats, the way she schedules her time, and the other activities she engages in are all designed to contribute to her fitness. Alice thus has no time for travel and eventually her friendships deteriorate because of neglect. Her exclusive and unwavering focus on one good thing has crowded out these other things of value. In this way, it can be said that Alice has overdone a good thing.

To be sure, Alice is no less physically fit for this fact. She very well may be *more* physically fit than she would have been had she also devoted due attention and effort to friendship and travel. We could even imagine that, as she's easily sidetracked, Alice's single-mindedness may have been crucial to her success at achieving her fitness goals. Thus the consuming nature of her pursuit is not self-undermining, at least not in the way we saw in the case of the cheesecake. Eating an eighth successive slice of cheesecake is positively displeasing; overdoing cheesecake undoes cheesecake's value. Things are different with the good of fitness. Overdoing fitness doesn't render one unfit. However, Alice has pursued physical fitness at the cost of certain other goods—friendship and travel— that she values. We might find this lamentable, judging that Alice has forsaken important goods for the sake of a good of relatively less value.

But Alice may not see things this way. She may reason—correctly, I should add—that all worthy pursuits impose costs, and sometimes among the costs of a valuable pursuit are other valuable pursuits. Maybe she is happy with the deal she has struck. Note, however, that this envisioned dispute with Alice concerns whether she has indeed overdone the good of fitness; the general good of fitness is not in question, nor is the idea that it is possible to overdo this good. Thus one can affirm the good of fitness while also recognizing the possibility of its overdoing.

Now let's introduce a complicating thought. One wonders what the *point* of Alice's focus on physical fitness might be, given that she has pursued it at the expense of other important things that she values. To be sure, part of the value of physical fitness has to do simply with the manifest goodness of being fit; it feels good to be physically fit. However, one might think that, in addition, the value of being physically fit is bound up with the incidence of other goods, such as socializing with friends and visiting new places. One might even go further and make the more general point that a large part of what's valuable about physical fitness is that it enables one to more fully pursue whatever else one thinks worthy.

As a quick survey at your local gym is likely to reveal, this thought accords with our practice. Typically, we pursue physical fitness for the sake of achieving, restoring, and maintaining health. And we want to be healthy so that we can engage in pursuits and projects of other kinds, projects that have as their point something other than our health. We pursue fitness so that we may engage in other valuable activities and pursue other goods, such as travel, socializing, and so on. Alice, however, has pursued fitness *at the expense of* all other pursuits.

For this reason, we are likely to regard Alice as obsessed or otherwise pathological. It's not merely that she has devoted herself entirely to a worthy project and thereby incurred the expense of abandoning certain other good pursuits; the crucial feature of Alice's situation is that she has devoted herself to a pursuit whose worth partly derives from the worth of certain other endeavors that it enables. In the absence of the pursuit of these other goods—friendships and enriching experiences, for example—the project of attaining physical fitness looks deranged. Alice's single-minded pursuit of fitness has not only crowded out other things of value; it also has crowded out goods the securing of which are part of what fitness is *good for*. Thus we might say that although Alice's consuming project of physical fitness does not involve the kind of self-defeat found in the cheesecake example, it nonetheless involves self-defeat of some kind. And we are right to think of this as a case of Alice overdoing a good.

To review, we have been exploring the question of how it could be possible to overdo a good thing. In the case of goods like cheesecake, there is a simple sense in which it is possible to overdo them. But there are good things of other kinds, and these goods can be overdone in a more complex sense. Some goods are overdone when our pursuit of them crowds out certain other significant goods. Moreover, sometimes when we overdo a good, we crowd out other goods whose achievement is part of the point of pursuing the good that is overdone. In these more complex cases, one can consistently affirm the especially high value of the overdone good, while calling for restraint in its pursuit.

Let's get back to democracy. Although important differences between it and Alice's fitness will be examined in Chapter 5, the case of Alice has helped us to glean a general way in which democracy may be a good that it is possible to overdo. We can do democracy in a way that crowds out other important social goods. I will argue later that when democracy is overdone, certain collateral social goods that must be secured in order for democracy to thrive are thereby smothered—not merely displaced, but neglected and caused to wither. In overdoing democracy, we undermine democracy. Thus my central thesis: Even in a democracy, politics must be kept in its place.

1.3 Too Much Democracy?

The claim that there could be too much democracy would be at most an idle curiosity unless it were a prelude to the further assertion that existing democracies are in fact overdoing it. The same goes for the related claim that democratic politics must be put in its place. After all, everything should be in its proper place, and thus the claim that democratic politics should put in its place would be nothing more than a vacuous platitude unless reasons were provided to hold that, in contemporary democracies, politics has overstepped its rightful bounds. In Chapter 3, I begin arguing for the more interesting idea: some contemporary democratic societies—the United States specifically—are indeed failing to keep politics in its place, and this is bad for democracy. But it must be emphasized once again that none of this expresses an antidemocratic sentiment. Quite the contrary! The view is that if they are to do democracy well, citizens must put politics in its place. Add to this that prevailing ills of contemporary democracy are largely the consequence of our overdoing of democracy.

Combining these thoughts together, one could say that if they are to do democracy well, citizens occasionally must retreat, together, from politics. They must devise avenues for cooperative social engagement that are in no way political, that do not have politics as their explicit purpose or objective. To turn a famous maxim from Jane Addams and John Dewey on its head, the cure for some of democracy's ills is to do *less*, not *more*, democracy.[1]

In fact, this reversal doesn't go far enough. Given that we are currently overdoing democracy, persisting steadfastly in political engagement under present conditions is likely to contribute centrally to democracy's corrosion. The instinctive disposition that prevails among many citizens across the political spectrum is to respond to current political ills with redoubled efforts at democratic action. Alas, this strategy is most likely doomed not only to fail, but also to backfire. If this is correct, then popular calls for increased participation in political activities designed explicitly to "reach across the aisle," establish "bipartisan" cooperation, or forge common ground across political divides are all ultimately insufficient, despite whatever value they might have in the more immediate political environment. In prescribing activities that are designed to surmount political divides, these calls still place politics at the center of the endeavor; hence they do not address the fundamental problem to which they are a response. If we seek to repair our democracy, we rather need to find other things to do together, things in which politics is not merely set aside, but instead has no place. We need to devise cooperative endeavors in which politics is not surmounted, but beside the point. Thus another slogan: If we want to do democracy well, we need sometimes to do something else entirely.

One may wonder what, precisely, is being recommended. What would it mean for citizens to engage together in cooperative endeavors that are not political in character? What could such endeavors be like? Responding to these questions in advance of the fuller argument of this book will be counterproductive; any proposal suggested at this point will strike the reader as already political in precisely the way to be eschewed. Still, something must be said. So, as a prelude, it may be helpful to mention trends that will be more fully discussed in Chapter 3.

The past thirty years have seen the gradual decline of traditional sites of activity in which people cooperated together without regard for political affiliation. Specifically, our workplaces, neighborhoods, places of worship, households, and shared public spaces have become both more politically homogeneous *and* more politically intoned. Although these spaces—workplaces in particular—used to serve as venues where citizens who might be politically divided could nonetheless work with each other and through those interactions come to regard one another as, say, a *dependable and skilled* coworker, *good neighbor*, or a *responsible parent*, they are progressively becoming settings in which individuals interact against the background of their salient political homogeneity. So our day-to-day social interactions are increasingly likely to put us in contact only with others who share our politics, and more and more of what we do together is regarded by us as also an expression of our politics. Our conceptions of a good neighbor, dependable coworker, and responsible parent are now likely to be infused with our political allegiances such that we gradually come to regard our political rivals as incapable of embodying these roles.

These trends are suggestive. But we must take care to not get ahead of ourselves. The present point is that in order to discern what it means to put politics in its place, we first need to understand how politics is being overdone. Accordingly, my account of what nonpolitical cooperative endeavors must wait until Chapter 5. However, it is worth calling attention here to the difficulty we have in imagining shared social activities in which politics plays no role. This difficulty is a symptom of the phenomenon this book aspires to identify and examine.

To be slightly more explicit, I will argue that part of what is involved in overdoing democracy is the tendency to conceptualize the entire social world as already claimed for projects that are irrevocably political; it is to regard the horizon of shared social endeavor as intrinsically saturated with politics. It is to conceive of the project of democratic self-government as omnipresent and all-embracing. Putting the point differently, it can be said that in overdoing democracy, we lose the capacity to regard our fellow citizens as anything other than citizens. We lose sensitivity to the fact that, in addition to being citizens, they are persons with ambitions, goals, and projects that extend beyond the travails of politics. Losing track of the fact that our political roles and responsibilities are not all-consuming makes for bad democracy. To employ yet another slogan: If we aspire to treat our fellow democratic citizens in the ways they ought to be treated, we must regard them as more than citizens.

The account thus far is likely to provoke the retort that although *politics* perhaps is being overdone in contemporary democracies, *democracy* is not. One may be tempted further to claim that our troubles lie in the combination of overdone politics and underdone democracy. What is needed, it will be said, is more democracy *instead of* politics. This reaction employs a distinction between democracy as a social ideal and democracy as a mere a mode of government; it then defines politics strictly as processes of government, and correspondingly identifies democracy with something beyond government, a social ideal that encapsulates all that is good, right, and wholesome in the social world. On such a view it is thus impossible to overdo democracy. Consequently, whatever ills may beset a democratic society, the source must lie in something other than democracy.

I agree that democracy is not merely a form of government, but is a far-reaching moral and social ideal. Nonetheless, democracy is an ideal that entails certain governmental forms, a particular politics, if you will. This entailment accounts for our tendency to regard certain institutions and processes as necessary for democracy; it similarly explains why we treat their absence from a specific social order as proof that the society is not democratic. In this way, the democratic moral and social ideal is not so easily detached from democracy's characteristic governmental forms after all. What's more, it follows from the claim that democracy is not *merely* a mode of government that democracy is *also* a mode of government. Accordingly, those who associate politics strictly with processes of government should in addition acknowledge that democracy is also a characteristic mode of politics. Thus when a democratic society overdoes its politics, it thereby overdoes democracy. The claim that although politics may be overdone in a democratic society, a society can never overdo democracy hence is confused.

To put the thought more directly, views that so starkly cleave apart democracy as a moral and social ideal from democracy's characteristic governmental forms attempt to dodge the problem identified in this book by definitional fiat. They begin from the brute stipulation that there could be no overdoing democracy. Perhaps there is some comfort to be had in this kind of verbal evasion. However, the problem identified in the coming chapters is in no way addressed by means of it.

Summing up, the core thesis of this book can be laid out in the following way. We are at present overdoing democracy, and democracy is suffering for it. Democracy is overdone when it is enacted in ways that crowd out other social goods that are necessary for democracy to thrive. When the whole of our shared social environment is organized around the projects, loyalties, and fractures of politics, we lose the capacity to treat our fellow citizens as anything other than political actors, either allies or obstacles to our political aims. However, in order to flourish, democracy needs citizens to be able to see one another as more than merely citizens. And if we are to regard our fellow citizens in this way, we need to put politics in its place. That is, we need sometimes to engage together in activities that are not already organized around or infused with politics.

I have not yet argued for any of these claims. I simply have been trying to explain what it means to say that democracy is being overdone and must be put in its place. Hopefully the thesis has been clarified. Still, the discussion thus far is likely to have provoked three important challenges that should be addressed directly. The first contends that the proposal is inherently conservative, acquiescent, and thus hostile to progressive political programs; accordingly, it challenges the *desirability* of putting politics in its place. The second questions the *possibility* of putting politics in its place by alleging that everything is political. The third challenges the proposal's democratic credentials, suspecting that the claim that democracy is being overdone is a prelude to the defense of a view that is frequently posed as a theory of democracy but in fact prescribes an *elitist* form of government. I'll take these up in turn.

1.4   Is the Thesis Conservative?

Some will object that the proposal sounds strikingly conservative, in the sense of being resigned and opposed to change.[2] The most common formulations of this objection claim that in collectively retreating from politics, we thereby acquiesce in the political status quo. Acquiescing in the status quo is tantamount to resigning ourselves to the injustice that prevails in contemporary democracies; thus acquiescence is tantamount to complicity. More than this, the envisioned critic will claim that the very idea of stepping back from politics is itself an exercise of political privilege, something possible only for those who are unjustly advantaged by the status quo.

These are serious allegations that I hope to dispel in the coming chapters. To make a start, though, I emphasize that what is being called for is neither political resignation, nor a full-scale withdrawal from politics. The proposal rather is that democratic citizens must make room for *occasionally* doing other things together, things not organized around our political allegiances. This is obviously consistent with high levels of explicitly political activity. And, to repeat, my claim is that unless one occasionally steps back, with others, in this way, one is likely to cause one's democratic endeavors to be counterproductive. Our steadfast political engagement could put vulnerable others at additional risk.

To explain: The cause of political justice is imperative. We struggle so vigorously in politics precisely because political decisions and policies affect real people, and can cause real suffering especially among those who are most socially vulnerable. We are morally required to act on their behalf. In a democracy, we pursue justice by means of political action. And in the face of especially egregious political failings, justice calls for especially exercised political engagements. None of this is being denied. The thesis that we must put politics in its place is consistent with a wholehearted devotion to social justice by means of democratic action. The prescription is not that when we engage in political action we should do *less* than what we presently are inclined to do. The claim rather is that alongside our political engagements, we need to reserve room for activities of other kinds, specifically cooperative social activities in which politics plays no part.

Recall that my contention is that overdoing democracy suffocates certain other social goods, and in particular it spoils the social goods that democracy requires in order to thrive. This book argues that, in the United States and elsewhere, we are overdoing democracy. If this is right, then continuing to overdo democracy is likely to exacerbate extant patterns of injustice; consequently, failing to put politics in its place threatens to endanger the most vulnerable among us. Those who persist in overdoing democracy of course might succeed in the short run in achieving their goals, but they do so at the broader expense of contributing to a thriving democracy. This renders their success pyrrhic; in attaining the desired political result, they have helped to sustain conditions under which all political outcomes are frail and volatile. Another slogan: In seeking a more just, egalitarian, and fair political order, our lives together must involve collective projects beyond these goals.

Still, it may be true that this prescription presupposes a certain degree of social privilege among my readers. I am not convinced that it does. But whether it does is of no consequence. The concession that such privilege is indeed presupposed occasions no objection to the thesis that politics must be put in its place. That various kinds of privilege exist may be objectionable, of course. But it does not follow that every action made possible by one's privilege is objectionable. There are certain activities that I am able to engage in only because of the advantages provided by my undeserved privilege; it does not follow that these very activities are themselves inappropriate exertions or impositions of that privilege.

Further, the idea that all actions made possible by objectionable privilege are ipso facto themselves objectionable is nearly certainly incoherent. Were it not for historical episodes of highly questionable moral standing, your forebears likely would never have met and you would never have been. Your existence is likely the product of undeserved privilege, if not severe injustice.[3] Or, to bring the matter more down to earth, that you are reading this book (or that you are able to read anything at all) is also an activity made possible by your privilege. Further, it is likely that your preferred modes of political action—donating, volunteering, demonstrating, organizing, marching, protesting, what have you—are possible because of privilege. In this way, the concern that putting politics in its place is possible only in the presence of unjust privilege threatens to expand into all areas of endeavor, condemning everything we might do—including our favored forms of vigilant political actions on behalf of justice.

To be clear, my view in no way denies that those who benefit from unjust arrangements have an obligation to effect political change in the direction of justice. It must be noted, though, that in order to do this, privileged persons must act in ways that are made possible by their privilege. More specifically, my claim is that in order to effect such change, democratic citizens must put politics in its place. If putting politics in its place requires privileged persons to perform acts that they can perform only because of their privilege, then so be it. Every political proposal imposes such requirements.

1.5 But Isn't *Everything* Politics?

Consider next a *conceptual* challenge. The thesis that we must put politics in its place requires that there is some realm of social life that lies outside of politics and is fundamentally apolitical. After all, if it is possible to put politics in its place, there must be some larger container within which to position it relative to other pursuits. And if it is possible to devise collaborative social endeavors in which politics plays no role, there must be some dimension of the social that is not itself political. Could there be such a dimension? Isn't it obvious that everything is politics?

The contention that "everything is politics" is intriguing. Statements of the form "everything is x" occasion certain notorious philosophical difficulties that we may set aside here.[4] In addressing the concern, it will be useful to distinguish two claims that might be advanced by someone who asserts that everything is politics.

First, one might be claiming that facts and considerations regarding the political order play a non-negligible role in *explaining* all aspects of our lives. This claim strikes me as surely correct. The full explanatory story about my typing this very sentence will invoke features of the political world I inhabit, and it must be conceded that had certain elements of that world been even slightly different, I would not be writing anything at all. Put more generally, for any of us, the most significant features of who we are cannot be explained without reference to events, institutions, norms, and structures that are irrevocably part of the political order. The upbringing, education, cognitive and emotional development, talents, struggles, projects, and achievements that constitute your biography can be made intelligible only by reference to certain facts about the political conditions under which you live.

Contrast this with a different claim that one might be making when asserting that "everything is politics." One might contend that the particular allegiances, profiles, loyalties, and struggles that occur within some given political context are *sufficient* to explain all facets of human life. This version of the claim is at work in certain notoriously misguided readings of Marxism, readings according to which no matter what one is doing, and no matter what one sincerely takes oneself to be doing, every action one performs is in fact motivated by and an expression of one's class identity. On this kind of view, it is obvious that there could be no putting politics in its place, because politics is the all-encompassing and ultimate explanation of all human things. The very idea of politics having a place to be put in is incoherent.

The first claim is both significant and true, while the second is neither. Everything is politics in the sense that political features of the world figure non-negligibly in the full explanation of any human phenomenon we're likely to think calls for explanation. The thesis that we must keep politics in its place is not at all threatened by this crucial insight. The project of putting politics in its place invokes no fantasy according to which we could stand apart from the political circumstances of our lives or disconnect from politics wholesale. More importantly, whatever possibilities there may be for devising venues for nonpolitical cooperative social activity will surely be a product of certain features of the political order within which we live. But recognizing that all explanations of human affairs must invoke facts about the prevailing politics is a far cry from embracing the claim that politics is the full explanation.

If you will tolerate a degree of terminological artificiality, the contrast is captured in the distinction between the claim that *everything is political* and the claim that *everything is politics*. Take the former to mean that political phenomena are part of the full account of any human behavior that stands in need of explanation. The latter is the quite different claim that all human behavior is politics, that politics is the complete explanation of everything about us. The former holds that reference to political phenomena cannot be eliminated from a proper explanation of human affairs; to repeat, this is a significant truth that is not inconsistent with my thesis. The latter contends that nothing other than politics is *necessary* for such an explanation. This doctrine strikes me as patently false. In any case, it is no less controversial than my thesis, and thus any critique launched from that quarter would need to offer a good deal of support for the premise.

Before moving on, it is worth reiterating that putting politics in its place is something we must do in order to rehabilitate democratic politics. It is thus a *political* endeavor in the sense just identified, even though it requires democratic citizens to retreat occasionally together from *politics*.

1.6 Oligarchy in Disguise?

An additional challenge to be considered here brings us back to the beginning of this chapter. The idea that democracy "has its place" and must not be "overdone" will strike the democrat's ear as the opening of a snobby discourse about the dangers of empowering the ignorant and gullible masses, and the corresponding need for the real power to be invested in a rational elite. To be sure, those who are familiar with the past century of democratic theory enjoy some warrant in suspecting that I am preparing the ground for a proposal whose democratic credentials are questionable. So-called *minimalist* theories of democracy begin from claims that admittedly sound akin to what I have been proposing, and minimalist views are widely regarded as barely democratic, if not positively oligarchic. That minimalist views are also known as *elitist* theories of democracy is suggestive.

The minimalist denies that any definite meaning can be given to the idea of popular self-government, and defends in its stead a conception of democracy as "that institutional arrangement for arriving at political decisions in which individuals acquire the power to decide by means of a competitive struggle for the people's vote."[5] Democracy on this view is simply an efficient mechanism for filling public offices and sustaining conditions under which the elected officials—the political "bosses"—are incentivized to exercise power moderately.[6] Central to this view is that once a democratic election takes place, the citizenry must withdraw from politics and attend to other things, lest they be guilty of "political back-seat driving."[7] In this way, the minimalist prescribes a kind of abstention from democratic politics and thus can be understood to be lamenting the tendency to overdo democracy. Furthermore, as the minimalist envisions a politics in which popularly selected elites rule, the view is often regarded, with some justification, as not really democratic at all.

The thesis that politics must be put in its place is different from the minimalist's view. Putting politics in its place does not require that citizens must stand back from democratic politics in order to provide sufficient room for elites to govern. Nor does it contain the claim that popular political power must be checked, and government shrunk, because of the appalling levels of political ignorance and irrationality that prevail among the citizenry.[8] The claim that current democratic societies are overdoing democracy is not about political power and who should hold it. It is rather about the infiltration of the categories, travails, allegiances, and rivalries of democratic politics into all aspects of our collective social experience. The call to put politics in its place is a call to try to reverse the saturation of social life by politics, to try to shrink somewhat the footprint of democratic politics on our shared social environment. To repeat, when democracy is all that we do together—when the political battles and loyalties of contemporary politics are permitted to structure every aspect of our shared civic life—other crucial social goods are smothered and democracy gets done badly. And when democracy is done badly, we all suffer.

1.7 Moving Forward

I trust that what has been said thus far is sufficient to show that the thesis that we must put politics in its place entails nothing that is antidemocratic or of questionable democratic pedigree. There is no inconsistency in holding the following four claims:

(i) Democracy is a capital, perhaps supreme, social good.
(ii) Proper democracy requires an engaged, active citizenry who regularly interact and reason together about the political issues of the day.
(iii) It is nevertheless possible to overdo democratic politics.

(iv) In contemporary democratic societies, politics is being overdone, and this is to the detriment of democracy.

Recall that putting politics in its place does not mean that when we engage in democratic politics, we must do less than what we are presently
inclined to do. The claim rather is that we must do more together than
engage in politics. And, to repeat, doing things together other than politics is necessary in order to do democracy well. So, once again, putting politics in its place is something we must do *especially* if we favor
a conception of democracy that prizes citizen engagement and public
activism. The thesis advanced here is thus unambiguously democratic.

That said, it will be argued in Chapter 5 that there are social and
interpersonal aims and aspirations whose value lies beyond politics. Accordingly, although the thesis that politics must be put in its
place will often be framed as something we must do in order to improve democracy, my claim is not that improving democracy must
be the aim of every activity we engage in, political and nonpolitical
alike. I suppose there are some among my readers who have already
put politics in its place simply by cultivating nonpolitical interests
that involve cooperation with others in contexts where politics is
regarded as simply irrelevant. It might be said of such citizens that
they have put politics in its place, but not for the sake of improving
democracy; they pursue their nonpolitical cooperative activities
simply out of interest and enjoyment. The argument of this book
in no way denounces this. In order to thrive, democracy needs us
to put politics in its place; however, this does not entail that putting
politics in its place is something we must enact with the intention of
improving democracy. In fact, it will be made evident in Chapter 5
that there is a sense in which we can put politics in its place only
by occasionally adopting as the point of our endeavors something
other than improving democracy.

An additional preliminary remark is in order before pressing
forward. The account presented in this book grows out of an

examination of a particular kind of dysfunction that has arguably beset contemporary democracy in the United States and elsewhere. The diagnosis and prescription are intended to apply only under circumstances where democracy, though faltering, is still sufficiently functional to warrant the commitment to trying to repair it from the inside, so to speak. Political conditions that are barely formally democratic or worse will obviously call for different palliative tools than those proposed here. Analysis of those tools, when their deployment is justified, and how we are to evaluate the degree of democratic commitment in a given social order are topics for another book.

I concede that everything remains uncomfortably vague. Crucial arguments are forthcoming. It will prove helpful to close this initial chapter with a sketch of how the argument will unfold.

The next item on the agenda is to make better sense of what democracy is, and why it is prone to being overdone. It will be argued in the next chapter that, whatever else one might say about democracy, it is a moral ideal, an image of proper political relations among citizens and between citizens and their government. It will be shown further that this moral ideal lends itself to various kinds of augmentation and expansion, leading to the idea that democracy is not merely a form of government or a system of politics, but also an embracing social order, a way of collective living beyond the mechanisms of government and policy. This will help establish that the democratic ideal itself drives us toward an expanding conception of the place of politics. Hence the problem of overdoing democracy is not a problem that arises out of a democratic lapse or departure; the problem rather is native to our democratic commitments.

Chapter 2 concludes Part I of this book, which is devoted to framing the thesis. With the lesson in hand that overdoing democracy is a tendency that is native to well-intentioned democratic citizens, I develop in Part II a more detailed diagnosis of how democracy has come to be overdone. This demonstration draws upon empirical materials regarding two closely related social phenomena that are ascendant and seemingly accelerating in many modern democracies, namely *political saturation* and *belief polarization*. The first is discussed in Chapter 3, where it will be argued that our social environments are politically homogeneous to an alarming degree and also are increasingly becoming sites for democratic politics. The upshot is that we are more than ever enacting our role as democratic citizens, but almost always under conditions that are themselves politically homogeneous, and thus not properly democratic. Appealing next to the widely documented phenomenon of belief polarization, Chapter 4 argues that political saturation is democratically *degenerative*, causing citizens to not only fall short of the democratic ideal, but to also grow progressively incapable of tracking it. In fact, it will be argued that even the most conscientious attempts to engage in properly democratic politics are liable to fuel the dysfunctions produced by belief polarization.

The grim diagnosis of Part II sets the stage for the prescription developed in Part III of the book. The argument of Chapter 5 returns to democratic theory, arguing that if democracy is to flourish, democratic citizens need to embody certain capacities. As it turns out, many of the requisite capacities are debilitated by belief polarization when it occurs under conditions of political saturation. What's more, it will be argued that the central democratic aptitudes—what I call the general capacity for *civic friendship*—can be developed only when citizens can step out of their political roles and interact as something other than citizens. In short, the flourishing of democracy depends upon citizens who manifest the capacity for civic friendship, but those very capacities are undermined when our social environments are politically saturated, and they can be cultivated only in nonpolitical social soil. From this follows the need to put politics in its place. After tendering a crucial caveat about making practical recommendations at a certain level of specificity, Chapter 5 proposes a strategy for putting politics in its place.

Despite the impression promoted by some of its most inspired enthusiasts, democracy is not the ultimate point of human life. This insight can be embraced even by those who, like myself, see democracy as the most important social good and as a necessary condition for the other capital political values, such as justice, equality, liberty, autonomy, and dignity. As great as democracy may be as an ideal, and as important its accompanying social values may be, we must not lose sight of the fact that the meaning and purpose of our lives does not lie exhaustively in the project of making democracy work. Democracy is a kind of social and political order, and like all orders of that kind it has a point and aspiration beyond itself. This theme is taken up in the concluding chapter, Chapter 6, where it will be argued that the problem of overdoing democracy in part arises from our tendency to lose track of the fact that, even supposing that its value is intrinsic, democracy nonetheless is *for something*, and that something is not simply more or even better democracy. I will make the case that the point of democracy is to foster valuable human relationships and lives that are devoted, collectively and individually, to meaningful projects that lie beyond the struggles of politics. If this is correct, then in failing to put politics in its place we not only contribute to the deterioration of a capital social good; perhaps even more importantly, we also lose touch with endeavors and aspirations that make life worthwhile.

2

Democracy's Expanding Reach

Readers will have noticed that although the previous chapter made continual reference to democracy, little has been said about what democracy is. So let's pause for a moment to think a bit about democracy. Start with a familiar textbook definition: democracy is rule by the people by means of votes and elected representatives, all constrained by a public constitution which recognizes individual rights. This formula gets a lot right, as far as it goes. But it really doesn't go very far. Notice that it provides no insight into what is arguably the basic democratic idea, namely, *rule by the people*. A moment's reflection on this idea provokes a swarm of philosophical questions, beginning with two that are most obvious: Who are the people? What does it mean for them to rule?

It would take several hundred pages to build this textbook definition into an adequately detailed philosophical conception of democracy. Our present purposes recommend that we begin elsewhere. What do we take ourselves to be doing when we are acting in our role as democratic citizens? What do those activities, when properly exercised, look like? More generally put: What is our ordinary, *workaday* understanding of democracy?

To be sure, as the textbook formulation acknowledges, voting in elections looms large in our ordinary view of what democracy is. However, it is also a component of our workaday conception that an election is the culmination of a campaign season. Campaigns involve multiple episodes of interaction between citizens, public officials, and those seeking political office. As democratic citizens, we vote in the wake of a season of debates, rallies, interviews, and speeches; and, crucially, we take voting to be a duty that is responsibly exercised only after having taken steps to become adequately informed about the issues, policies, and candidates set before the citizenry. We might say, then, that our workaday conception of democracy invokes a duty for citizens to participate in certain kinds of political activities in advance of exercising their political power by casting a vote. And this is why modern democracy is awash with forums and occasions for citizens to engage with each other and with public officials on matters of common concern. Importantly, these forums are frequently organized around the idea that democratic rule is the rule of *reasons*. That is, we understand democratic citizenship to call for something other than haggling or bargaining for one's favored political outcome; when we act as democratic citizens, we are supposed to be attending to the reasons that count for and against various political decisions and policies. In this way, democratic citizenship involves exercises of judgment, rather than simply expressions of preference. And it is because democratic decision-making is meant to be driven by reasons that citizens are able to question, criticize, challenge, support, and defend their political views; it is also what enables them to hold their representatives accountable.

Of course, this brisk depiction captures democracy as an *ideal*. In the real world, democratic practice rarely lives up to this conception. However, note that the image just sketched presents a common aspiration we have as democratic citizens in that we take our own political views to be based in reasons, just as we take the views of those with whom we disagree to be ill-informed, misguided, and correctable. Furthermore, notice that popular diagnoses of what's going wrong with contemporary democracy tend to assume an ideal of precisely the sort just presented. When we object to the commanding role that money and privilege play in our democracy, we are often affirming that democratic politics should rather be directed by reasons. And when we lament the ways in which social media can be deployed to disseminate misinformation, propaganda, and "fake news," we are also affirming the idea that in a democracy citizens must be adequately informed. Thus it turns out that our ordinary conception of democracy invokes the ideal of a citizenry that participates together in thinking critically about the political issues of the day.

This chapter develops this workaday understanding of democracy in greater detail. In order to do this we will need to see how this ideal emerges out of simpler and more austere conceptions of what democracy is. Thus we will need here to trace a certain progression in democratic theory. It should be emphasized, though, that the point of the discussion is not simply to better capture our workaday conception in a way that reveals its connections to the trajectory of democratic theory. The objective rather is to establish that the origin of the problem of overdoing democracy is not external to democracy. It comes from the inside, so to speak. By charting the path of contemporary democratic theory, we can understand how the democratic ideal itself urges us to embrace practices that can lead us to overdo politics. Acknowledging this internal tendency is to take an important step towards rehabilitating democratic politics; specifically, seeing the problem as endemic prevents one from adopting certain popular prescriptions for repairing democracy that are bound to backfire. Thus another slogan: Recognizing that democracy inclines toward its overdoing can help prevent us from causing its undoing.

Chapter 1 employed a curious series of metaphors relating to the place, extension, and space of democracy. Cashing these out is the first order of business at present. After introducing some new conceptual material to replace these metaphors, I will argue that the enterprise of understanding democracy requires us to think of democracy as a *social ideal*, and this in turn encourages expanding conceptions of democratic political practice.

2.1 Scope, Site, and Reach

We start again at square one. Any theory of democracy needs to identify the activities, processes, and interactions that are characteristic of democratic governance. In addressing these, theorists devise detailed accounts of the various political institutions that make up a democracy, including constitutions, methods of representation, electoral systems, judicial bodies, and so on. But, as democracy is on any view fundamentally a system of *self-government among citizens*, no account can be complete without a specification of the duties, obligations, and responsibilities that fall within the distinctive office of democratic citizenship. Call this specification the *scope* of democracy. Different conceptions of democracy tend to offer competing accounts of democracy's scope.

Generally, a conception of democracy's scope is a view of what it takes to be a properly functioning democratic citizen. This involves a view of what citizens *must do* in order to contribute to democracy, as well as views of what it would be *good, admirable*, or *exemplary* for them to do, in their role as citizen. Accordingly, any view of democracy's scope also will entail a conception of when a democratic citizen is deserving of criticism or even derision or reproach. To take an example already mentioned, nearly every view of democracy includes in its conception of democracy's site the action of voting. Few would deny that a central duty of democratic citizenship is voting in political elections. Hence voting is regarded nearly always as an admirable action for a democratic citizen to perform; similarly, neglecting to vote is typically regarded as a dereliction of one's duty as a citizen, and therefore worthy of criticism. In several modern democracies voting is mandatory, and failing to vote is (mildly) punished. And one reasonably might be inclined to regard one who *sells* her political power as not merely criticizable, but contemptable as a citizen.

Although nearly every theory of democracy includes voting as an activity that is central to democracy's scope, most incorporate a more robust view than this. They include within democracy's scope various activities that are closely related to voting, such as following or participating in political campaigns, canvassing for candidates, volunteering at polling places, and contributing in other ways to electoral processes. Some views take a step further and contend that activities related to acquiring and processing the kind of political information that could *inform* one's voting—following the news, attending to debates over public policy, studying the policy platforms of the candidates and parties, and so on—are also part of democracy's scope. These theories include among the duties of citizenship actions that would enable one to be a responsible voter. Other views embrace still more extensive conceptions; they include within democracy's scope activities that go beyond those associated with elections, including community involvement, charitable giving, volunteering for social causes, and so on.

We can sum up by saying that a view of democracy's scope is a view of the range of activities that it is part of the office of democratic citizenship to perform or participate in. When a citizen engages in an activity that falls within the assigned scope of democracy, he or she is properly said to be contributing to the distinctive business of democratic politics. Thus her performance in that activity can be assessed from the perspective of the duties and responsibilities that attach to the role of being a democratic citizen.

Now, some of the activities specified within a conception of democracy's scope are understood to be *required* of democratic citizens, and thus those who perform them badly, or who omit them entirely, are thereby subject to criticism as a citizen. Other activities within the scope are held not to be requirements, but something more akin to *expectations*. Those who engage in such activities should do them well (and are subject to criticism qua citizen for doing them badly), but generally those who omit them entirely are not thereby deserving of criticism. Of course, on any view, the boundary within democracy's scope between the required and (merely) expected will be fluid. Think, for instance, of the conflicting ideas regarding military service that one finds within existing democracies. In some democracies, military service is mandatory for all citizens, and in others it is (merely) expected, seen as a thing that citizens ought to do. Elsewhere service is regarded as simply admirable. And there are times and places where serving in the military has been regarded as something to be criticized.

In addition, every view of democracy also will countenance, perhaps only implicitly, some class of activity that falls outside of democracy's scope. That is to say, on every conception of democracy, there will be certain actions that democratic citizens may perform that in no way invoke their office as citizen, and so are not appropriately evaluated in those terms. For example, democratic citizens tend to take up hobbies and pastimes of various kinds—they play piano, collect comics, watch movies, follow sports, bake cakes, write poetry, work on cars, garden, woodwork, coach kids, hike, knit, brew their own beer, and so on—and these activities generally lie outside of their office as democratic citizens. To be sure, some citizens take up hobbies that have significant value and may contribute importantly to the collective good of society, while others devote time to more strictly personal endeavors. What places all of these activities normally outside of the scope of democracy is that whether they are done well or badly—or even done at all—does not matter strictly from the perspective of democratic citizenship. Gardening might contribute importantly to the social good, but no one is to be criticized, as a citizen, for not having a garden. And being an awful pianist, cook, or knitter could render one deserving of criticism, but not in the role of *citizen*. Again, different conceptions of democracy's scope will naturally embrace different views of which activities lie beyond the office of citizen. Observe again that within any conception of democracy, the precise border between that which lies inside and outside of democracy's scope will also be variable.

To get a flavor of how the boundary concerning democracy's scope is contested, consider ongoing disputes over childrearing. No one denies that abusive parenting is a serious violation; it's obvious that the state must protect children, and there is also a sense in which being at least a decent parent is in some measure a responsibility of citizenship. But think of controversies over homeschooling and certain forms of religious education. For example, in the well-known case of *Mozert v. Hawkins County*, evangelical parents objected to a public school's reading curriculum and sought an accommodation by which they could homeschool the reading portion of the public education curriculum.[1] The parents argued that, as the primary-grade textbooks that were being used included readings from the perspectives of several different faiths (including non-Christian faiths), the school was exposing their children to the dangerous doctrine of moral and religious relativism, and thereby imperiling their souls. The *Mozert* case is fascinating, and part of what makes it so is that it calls into question the nature of the boundary between the elements of parenting that fall within democracy's scope and those that fall outside.

Turn next to democracy's *site*. We have already seen, albeit implicitly, that the different views of democracy's scope—the distinctive activities constitutive of the office of democratic citizenship—also identify various places where democracy "happens" or is "enacted." These are the spaces, both physical and social, where activity can rightly be regarded as contributing to democratic governance. The collection of such spaces is the *site* of democracy.

To revert to our earlier example, according to nearly every view of democracy, the activity of voting falls centrally within democracy's scope; consequently, it is common to think that one central place where democracy happens is in voting booths on Election Day. Thus, nearly everyone agrees that democracy's site includes polling places, and also the physical spaces immediately surrounding them. Those views that embrace more robust conceptions of democracy's scope will tend to involve correspondingly more robust understandings of its site. For example, theories of democracy that regard activities aimed at acquiring and processing political information as falling within the scope of democracy will tend to include within democracy's site spaces like public libraries, television studios, and radio stations.

Views of this kind that in addition embrace more sophisticated accounts of the epistemological issues concerning the transmission and accessing of political information will also embrace certain understandings of the nonphysical spaces that constitute democracy's site. They will tend to theorize democracy as a "space of reasons,"[2] or what might be called a certain kind of social-epistemic environment. And, as one would expect, those who place within democracy's scope activities of face-to-face interaction, community involvement, public dialogue, and various modes of social gathering will also tend to recognize parks, street corners, community centers, cafés, pubs, and interactive regions of the Internet as part of democracy's site.

Recognizing a space as belonging to the site of democracy does not necessarily mark it as *exclusively* for democratic activity, nor does it entail that whatever may happen in that space thereby counts as part of democratic politics. To be sure, certain spaces are exclusively for democratic activity—think of voting booths, jury rooms, and courthouses. But many locations within democracy's site will be intrinsically multipurpose, spaces where political and nonpolitical activity can coexist, sometimes simultaneously. For instance, on Sunday mornings in the park next to my home one can find Frisbee playing, picnicking, and sunbathing, all occurring alongside various forms of political petitioning. The petitioners are exercising the office of citizenship while the Frisbee players, picnickers, and sunbathers are not. The public park is located within democracy's site, even though not everything that occurs there counts as an exercise of democratic citizenship.

In identifying a public park as a space within democracy's site, one claims that it is a place where political activity can commence or be initiated. It is perhaps also to say that political activity is generally to be *welcome* there. Consequently, one also affirms that when activity that falls within democracy's scope commences in a space within democracy's site, individuals are to be regarded as acting in their office of citizenship, and thus they rightly can be engaged as citizens, and held to the standards of proper citizenship. In other words, given any particular conception of democracy, when an individual performs acts that fall within democracy's scope in a space that is located within democracy's site, he or she may be criticized or praised—more generally, held to account—for the performance *qua* citizen.

To repeat, on any view of these matters, the precise borders of democracy's scope and site will be arguable, and one should expect a certain degree of plasticity in every account. Like borders of other kinds, the scope and site of democracy will themselves be susceptible to critique and calls for redrawing. However, one intuitive line of demarcation is suggested by current democratic practice. Specifically, we tend to hold that social contexts where it would be difficult or impossible for citizens to hold each other to the standards of citizenship should be regarded as lying outside of democracy's site.

To see this, consider a space that is typically—and I think rightly—regarded as beyond democracy's site, namely the holiday dinner table. Familial bonds affect interactions in ways that are notoriously vexed, as venerable genres of drama and comedy attest. Holidays involve intense gatherings of family members who may not interact regularly, and might not have much in common, but are nonetheless bound together as family and thus cannot easily disassociate from one another. Political statements made over a holiday dinner are generally, and rightly, regarded as out of place, especially when they're controversial among those in the room to whom they are addressed. Provoking a political wrangle over holiday dinner is typically regarded as bad form. And this is not simply because disputes of this kind tend to be unpleasant. Rather, the thought is that political disputation belongs elsewhere, in a context where the disputants can interact fully and freely in their role as citizens.

Those who violate this general rule are thought to be boorish and impolite, and perhaps moral failures deserving of severe rebuke, but not thereby failures as democratic citizens. Indeed, one can uphold the view that the holiday dinner table lies beyond democracy's site while also embracing the view that vigorous political debate is a central activity within democracy's scope. In some other space or at some other occasion in that location, the jarringly partisan pronouncements of your opinionated uncle might be perfectly acceptable. But at holiday dinner, those very statements are out of bounds. The suggestion here is that political statements are out of bounds in contexts, such as holiday dinners, where those subjected to them, those to whom they are addressed, are unable to engage with them fully as citizens.

Similar analyses are available about political activities in other spaces. Workplaces and classrooms are properly held to be spaces where certain activities that fall clearly within democracy's scope are nonetheless out of place. When those activities nonetheless are enacted in those spaces, they are inappropriate.

So imagine an office where every day the boss broadcasts throughout the entire workspace the political speeches of her favorite politician, or a college classroom where a professor spends the first ten minutes of each meeting stumping for his favored candidate in an upcoming election. To be sure, there is a good deal that is problematic in each of these cases. But part of what is objectionable is that otherwise permissible (and possibly admirable) political advocacy is occurring within a space where citizens cannot really treat each other as citizens. The workers and the students are being politically addressed in a context where they cannot engage as citizens otherwise should. So, the workers and the students who oppose the political messaging to which they are subjected, or even wish merely to question it, cannot really voice their objections and questions; or at least they cannot do so without risking retaliation from the boss or professor. To put the point more generally, workplaces and classrooms generally are not spaces where open political discussion and deliberation among equal citizens can commence. There is other work to do there, after all. Moreover, while individuals are occupying those spaces, they are bound by relations other than those that constitute citizenship. Political debate within a workplace is always in part debate among individuals *qua* boss and employee, manager and subordinate; and in schools, although students and professors may in certain classes engage in political debate, their activity there is circumscribed and directed by the pedagogical mission of the classroom and course.

Consider another example. Recently the National Football League introduced a sanction against those players who opt to "take a knee" while on the field during the playing of the national anthem prior to NFL football games. The analysis we have been exploring provides an account of why this policy is misplaced. Standing in attention, with hand on heart, while the anthem is played is an action that constitutes an official expression of one's loyalty to one's country; it is for this reason an act of citizenship. Perhaps it is a duty of citizenship to stand in attention when the anthem is played. But if the playing of the anthem invokes a duty of citizenship, situations where it is played must also be taken to be contexts in which other political activities must be permitted, including especially certain acts of peaceful, nondisruptive, and legal protest. As in the workplace example mentioned, the football stadium is a workplace for the players, and if their employer sees fit to call for an act of citizenship, it must also allow for other acts of citizenship, including (peaceful, nondisruptive, legal) action aimed at political critique.

Those who object to the practice of kneeling during the playing of the anthem on the grounds that it "politicizes" the football game must notice that as the games begin with a performance of the national anthem, and thus with the corresponding duty on the part of all citizens present to stand, the occasion has been already rendered political. If that call to citizenship occurs in a space that cannot accommodate peaceful, nondisruptive, and legal acts of expressing political critique, the call is misplaced. Those who oppose the kneeling should also oppose the playing of the national anthem.

The workplace and classroom examples show that permissible acts of citizenship can be rendered inappropriate when performed in the wrong spaces; the NFL example affords an instance in which it is alleged that an otherwise permissible act of citizenship (expressing a critique of existing trends in policing) is unwelcome in a sports arena during a moment marked out for an act of citizenship. We easily can add to our catalogue of examples cases where everyday activities that fall outside of democracy's scope are misdirected when performed within strictly democratic spaces. Imagine Bible study among jurors during deliberation in a jury room, or OTB-style gambling about election outcomes in polling places on Election Day. Note further that certain forms of protest consist in performing political acts in what are commonly regarded as nonpolitical spaces. And there are other forms of protest that enact nonpolitical behavior in political spaces, too. Often what makes these activities legible to us as *protest* is that they are out of place.

We need not pursue these matters any further. The point has been simply to note that a theory of democracy needs to incorporate accounts of the scope and site of democracy. That is, part of what a conception of democracy must do is provide an account of *what activities* are characteristic or distinctive of the office of democratic citizenship, and *where* those activities are typically to be enacted or performed. Introducing an additional term now, we can say that the combination of a given conception of democracy's view of the site and scope of democracy is its view of democracy's *reach*. Roughly, for any conception of democracy, the richer the conceptions of scope and site it involves, the broader its view of democracy's reach.

These concepts provide a less impressionistic formulation of the central thesis of this book. Consider: contemporary democratic societies have embraced a hyperextended conception of democracy's reach. They have adopted a conception of democracy's scope that allows for the attribution of political significance—and accountability qua citizen—to too much of what people do, and accordingly tends to recognize too many spaces as sites in which democratic citizenship is to be enacted. And, to recall to our main theme, when all modes of social interaction are understood to be enactments of democratic citizenship, we overdo democracy in the ways specified in the previous chapter—we come to see one another *solely* as political agents who either obstruct or help enable our own political projects. Seeing our fellow citizens strictly as citizens leads us to interact with them in ways that dissolve the other social goods that democracy requires if it is to flourish. In putting politics in its place, we must impose constraints on democracy's reach.

Constraining democracy's reach is consistent with embracing a very broad conception of the proper scope and site of democracy. What is being called for is the denial that democracy's reach is *boundless*. As I will argue in the next chapter, currently we are overdoing democracy in that politics has become practically inescapable. Democratic politics has infiltrated and now saturates the whole of our shared social environment. The need to put politics in its place is the need to reclaim regions of the social sphere for cooperative projects that do not invoke the office of citizenship.

It is important to recognize, though, that the political predicament we find ourselves in is not due to a democratic failing or the infiltration of nondemocratic ideals into our politics. The problem of overdoing democracy arises out of democracy itself, out of democratic theory and practice. This is why the solution to the problem is not more or even better democracy. In order to see this, it is necessary to canvass some trends in democratic theory. The argument of the remaining sections of this chapter will be that if we are to capture the fundamental ideal of a democratic society in a plausible depiction of a political order, we must ascribe to democracy an expansive reach. Acknowledging this point about democratic theory is crucial for showing how democratic practice tends toward overextending its reach.

2.2 Democracy as a Social Ideal

Democracy is an answer to a particular moral problem. Politics inevitably involves the establishment of rules (in the form of policies, laws, procedures, edicts, and the like) to which members of a given population are subject. And, given even a modestly sized population, for any set of rules that may be established politically, there will be some among those subject to the set who prefer alternative arrangements, different rules. Consequently, politics also inevitably involves the *enforcement* of rules. And enforcement requires the exercise of coercive power directed toward securing compliance with the rules and punishing noncompliance. A system of government is said to be legitimate when it is *entitled* to exercise the coercive power necessary to enforce its rules. Now, if one affirms—with Plato and Aristotle, among others in the history of political thought—that persons naturally stand in relations of hierarchy to one another and thus are not equals, politics as such poses no distinctive *moral* problem. According to views of this kind, the main challenge of politics is the practical one of placing the right people in charge.

However, once one embraces the idea that all persons are equals and hence rejects the idea of natural hierarchy, politics presents a moral problem all its own. How is legitimate political rule possible? As persons are equals, how could any subset of them, or any institution that they might devise, be entitled to exercise coercive power over them all? How could a political body rightfully enforce decisions among a population of equals when some in the population reject those decisions? Recall the philosophical anarchist mentioned briefly at the start of Chapter 1. The anarchist claims that wherever there's politics, there's the exercise of power aimed at forcing people to comply with rules that they reject, and that means that politics necessarily involves circumstances where some boss others around. How could political bossing possibly be consistent with the idea that everyone is an equal? The philosophical anarchist answers that no system of politics is consistent with moral equality; anarchism thus denies that political rule is ever justifiable.

Democracy is the proposition that political rule can be made consistent with the fundamental moral equality of all persons; it is the claim that legitimate government among moral equals is indeed possible. The broad idea is suggestively articulated by Jean-Jacques Rousseau, who saw democracy as "a form of association . . . by means of which each one, while uniting with all, nevertheless obeys only himself and remains as free as before."[3] This can be put more plainly by saying that democracy is the proposition that each person's status as an equal is preserved in a system of government that affords to each citizen an equal say in deciding the political rules by which all citizens will live. Of course, it remains to be discerned what it means for each to have an equal say and what kinds of rules are properly political; naturally these are central debates in contemporary democratic theory. For now we can distill matters by identifying democracy with the *social ideal* of a self-governing community of political equals.

2.3 Capturing the Ideal: The Classical Approach

The philosophical disputes over democracy that I just mentioned involve competing accounts of what it would take for a social and political order to instantiate the democratic ideal, what would have to be the case for a given social and political arrangement to qualify as one in which equals collectively govern themselves. My aim at present is to show how the attempt to adequately capture the democratic ideal in a workable theory of politics leads naturally to an expanding conception of the reach of politics. Putting politics in its place partly involves recognizing this tendency within the democratic ideal.

To begin, then, we are all familiar with one account of when the democratic ideal is realized. This view holds that self-government among equals is achieved when, with respect to any collective decision, each individual who will be bound by the decision gets exactly one vote, each votes his or her preference, the votes are equally counted, and the majority rules. Call this familiar view *equal-vote majoritarianism*. Of course, large-scale democracies are far more complex in their collective decision-making processes than this suggests. Modern democracies employ systems of political representation, and this means that most laws and policies are not decided by a popular vote, but by processes involving elected representatives, and many of these processes are not strictly majoritarian. To further complicate matters, some contemporary democratic theorists argue for decision-making arrangements that deviate from equal-vote majoritarianism. Among these, some argue for a weighted or "plural" system that gives some citizens greater voting power than some of their fellows;[4] others argue in favor of various forms of electoral lottery, where only a subset of the citizens are enfranchised for any given election.[5]

These are intriguing proposals that we can set aside. Among democrats, any departure from the simple system of equal-vote majoritarianism stands in need of special justification. Deviations can be rendered consistent with democracy if they can be shown either to be products of an equal majoritarian vote, or otherwise necessary in preserving the democratic order and protecting democratic citizens. That is to say that equal voting with majority rule is the fundamental democratic *default*. The question we need to address is whether equal-vote majoritarianism is indeed sufficient as a basic conception of self-government among political equals.

So let's begin with a simplistic case. Three friends—Ann, Betty, and Cara—wish to go to the movies together tonight. Their local cinema is showing two films; one is a bittersweet romantic comedy, and the other is an action-packed thriller. Imagine that Ann, Betty, and Cara are not indifferent with respect to which film to see, and neither are they of one mind about the choice. How should they decide? There's something undeniably attractive about the thought that they should each state their preferred movie, and the group should go to whichever film the majority wants to see. Of course, at least one member of the group will be made to see a different movie from the one she prefers, but each member of the group had an equal say in the collective decision. Isn't that democracy?

As it is the simple view of democracy that we learn as children, call this the *schoolyard view*. We tend to appeal intuitively to this view in decision-making contexts of nearly all kinds; it strikes us expedient and patently fair to all parties affected by a collective choice. Much of classical democratic theory contends that a suitably elaborated version of this general picture is sufficient for capturing the democratic ideal in a system of large-scale political governance.

The trouble is that once a few minor complexities are introduced into a decision-making situation, the schoolyard view loses much of its intuitive force. For example, suppose Ann *really* wants to see the romantic comedy and really dislikes thrillers, whereas Betty and Cara have only a slight preference in favor of the thriller, but are not opposed to the romantic comedy. Or consider the possibility that Ann's preference for the romantic comedy is the result of her having read several reviews by reliable critics, whereas Betty's and Cara's preference for the thriller is not informed by reviews, or anything at all for that matter. Further, imagine that Ann's preference for the romantic comedy is based on reliable reviews and expresses her educated judgment concerning which film Betty and Cara are most likely to enjoy, whereas Betty and Cara have a robust track record of picking movies that they wind up not enjoying. Next, imagine a case in which Ann strongly prefers the romantic comedy, and Betty strongly prefers the thriller, but Cara decides to put her own preference aside and votes for the thriller because she knows that Betty, unlike Ann, will get angry if she votes against the thriller. Or consider the case in which Ann realizes that both Betty and

Cara are in some significant way *misinformed* about the thriller; suppose that they mistakenly believe that it stars their favorite actor and has an uplifting and patriotic message, while Ann knows that it stars an unknown actor and ends with a bleak embrace of existential dread. Finally, imagine that Ann wants to see the romantic comedy, and Betty wants to see the thriller, but Betty, knowing that Cara will vote only for a film that stars her favorite actor, tricks Cara into voting for the thriller by lying to her about who its star is. In any of these instances, does the schoolyard view instantiate self-government among equals? It seems not.

The schoolyard view can be made to lose its luster pretty swiftly. It bears repeating that we are still considering simplistic cases. Difficulties multiply quickly once further complexity is introduced. One only needs to envision a slightly larger group of filmgoers with a greater number of options in order to generate a range of new difficulties. More importantly, though, observe that democratic politics is crucially unlike a group decision among filmgoers in that the former involves the exercise of coercive power and the latter does not. In a democracy—unlike in a group of filmgoers—one cannot simply opt out of the group if it decides against one's preference. When democracy decides, we are presumptively all bound by the outcome, and we render ourselves liable to enforcement—including punishment—if we do not comply.

Now, classical theories of democracy attempt to address some of these difficulties by adding to equal-vote majoritarianism various institutional measures; these include the familiar constitutional constraints, modes of representation, and schemes of individual rights that figure into the workaday conception from which we started. These are touted as protections against the system's most severe defects. And that is correct, as far as it goes. However, the point remains that the schoolyard view has it that individuals are treated as equals—given an "equal say" in deciding the collective rules—when they are afforded the same number of votes, and thus the same chance to have their preference transformed into policy.

Yet it is obvious that "one person, one vote" is not sufficient for treating individuals as equals in a system of government. More specifically, the schoolyard view understands equality simply as equality of *input*, but this kind of equality is arguably consistent with various forms of political and social inequality.

Consider that equal-vote majoritarianism renders democracy consistent with a background culture in which vast inequalities—of power, standing, resources, influence, and the like—are prevalent. Under cultural conditions like these, it seems plausible to think that equal voting is not sufficient for having an equal say in the decision-making process. That is, a community might make its collective decisions by means of a system of equal-vote majoritarianism and yet fail to plausibly instantiate the democratic ideal. Thus equal-vote majoritarianism is insufficient to capture the democratic ideal. Democracy must involve something more.

In light of this result, our thinking about democracy reaches a crossroads where we must choose between two quite different theoretical paths. Along one path lies the minimalist conception that was discussed in the previous chapter. This view, you will recall, dissolves the idea of self-government among equals into a conception of democracy according to which it is nothing more than an effective mechanism for producing stable nonauthoritarian government. The other path retains the ideal of self-government among equals, but seeks to address the shortcomings of equal-vote majoritarianism by supplementing it with a more robust conception of democracy's reach.

Now, although minimalism remains a viable option in contemporary political theory, it will not be addressed here. The minimalist program is driven by the claim that more robust conceptions of democracy are either incoherent or implausible; many of minimalism's advocates take its chief virtue to be that it is really the only game in town, so to speak. One wonders how many minimalists would opt for a minimalist view in the presence of a recognizably workable nonminimalist alternative. In any case, the second kind of response to the insufficiency of equal-vote major-itarianism is what's important for our purposes, as it reflects the path along which democratic practice has in fact traveled.

2.4 The Need for Public Engagement

Views along this second path emphasize that democracy is fundamentally the kind of *society* against which equal-vote majortarianism could function as an adequate method of collective political decision-making for a community of equals. In such a society, each citizen must be afforded not only an equal vote, but also an equal *voice* among fellow citizens. We might say, then, that in order to capture the democratic ideal, one must adopt a *public engagement* conception of democratic society. The question then becomes what kind of engagement is called for.

One might begin developing a public engagement conception by thinking that democracy requires widespread participation in the tasks that are related to collective self-government. Participation of the kind envisioned encourages citizens to see themselves as sharers in a common civic project; by participating in this endeavor, citizens put aside their interests as private individuals and, together with others, adopt the perspective of the whole political community, acting for the sake of the common good.[6] Democracy hence is envisioned as equal-vote majoritarianism conducted against the backdrop of a large-scale collection of interlocking civic associations, where individuals come together not as adversaries with competing interests, but as fellow citizens pursuing the distinctive good of the whole. Thus the emphasis is transferred away from the need to produce collective decision amidst conflicting preferences and toward civic processes aimed at fomenting solidarity, community, mutual understanding, and a sense of belonging among citizens.

The participationist image of a socially engaged community of collaborators seems to capture nicely the ideal of self-government among equals because it suggests that properly democratic decisions are the products of public-spirited engagement among varying political coalitions and groups. On the participationist model, when one's side loses the vote, one can nonetheless take solace in the fact that one's fellow citizens enacted public-minded activities and simply took a different view from one's own of the common good. And what's more, on this view it is central to democracy that public-spirited engagement continue after the votes are counted. Thus those who find themselves on the losing side of a vote may still engage in social and political activities designed to convince their fellow citizens to reverse their decision; one may continue to organize, criticize, challenge, and, in some cases, even resist and protest the prevailing decision. In this way, the participationist model holds that no citizen is simply *subjected* to an outcome he or she opposes. Even though one might be forced to comply, one nevertheless retains one's status as an equal citizen who may continue to politically advocate on behalf of the losing option.

It is clear that the participationist model better captures the democratic ideal than the schoolyard view can. But it should also be obvious that participationism involves a significant expansion of democracy's reach. On standard versions of this view, the site of democracy includes the whole of public space, and its scope encompasses a broad range of activities that citizens might engage in collectively, from typical political undertakings surrounding campaigns and legislation to various kinds of broader social action, including community organizing, neighborhood development, conscience-raising, consumer advocacy and even bowling together in leagues.[7]

Yet the participatory model still may not be sufficient to address adequately the problems that were raised with the schoolyard view. The activities of organizing and building coalitions are surely a central element of the democratic process; moreover, the kind of civic-minded activity prescribed by participationism is without a doubt necessary for a healthy democracy. But there remain difficulties in cases where the broader culture tends to ignore or disregard the ideas, concerns, and voices of some citizens, even when they are well-organized and speaking out. When certain segments of the citizenry are subjected to systematic marginalization and denigration, the fact that they are afforded opportunities to publicly organize amounts to only a small improvement over the classical model. Where social standing is unequal due to the prevalence of subtle but durable bigotry, discrimination, and unjust bias lurking in the background culture, the participatory conception offers little remedy.

One might press further in this direction and argue that the participationist places the onerous task of democratic progress squarely on those segments of the population that are likely to be the least powerful, and, not incidentally, also the most vulnerable. To put the point in another way, the participationist conception encourages citizens—both as individuals and as groups—to speak up, but it does not ensure that anyone actually listens. It is difficult to see how such a conception realizes the ideal of self-government among equals.

Thus although adding to the schoolyard view a conception of participation may be necessary to capture the democratic ideal, it is not sufficient; other conditions must be added. Hence we may need to thicken our conception of public engagement. One might think that in order to realize self-government among equals, citizens must be afforded not only equal votes and an equal voice, but also an equal *hearing*.[8] This suggests that the democratic ideal calls for a social order in which, among the other modes of public engagement, citizens are expected to communicate together in certain ways, ways that include not only speaking, but also listening and perhaps in addition inviting and welcoming others to speak.[9]

Deliberative conceptions of democracy propose that the ideal of self-government among equals is realized when democratic outcomes are in some sense the product of *public deliberation*. Hence deliberativists share with participationists the idea that democracy is more than campaigns, voting, and elections. Like participationism, deliberativism holds that the social and civic processes leading up to and following an election are crucial elements of democracy's reach. Deliberative democrats also embrace the participationist vision of a vibrant and dynamic civil sphere, active with social and political organizations, associations, and undertakings of all kinds. But the deliberativist adds to this a distinctive concern with the ways citizens form their political views and the reasons that inform citizens' votes and other activities.

The central deliberativist thought is that, in a democracy, collective decisions derive their authority from the fact that, prior to voting, each citizen was able to engage in processes whereby he or she could rationally persuade others to adopt his or her favored view by defending it with reasons, and offering reasons opposing competing views. According to the deliberativist, then, the democratic ideal has at its core an idea of *collective reasoning*.[10] In order for citizens to rule themselves as equals, they must reason together as equals.

Admittedly, that sounds lofty. But the deliberative model nonetheless offers a compelling theoretical resolution of the moral problem that democracy is meant to address. To see this, imagine that a citizen named Frances finds herself on the losing end of a democratic vote over an issue that is important to her. Frances hence is expected to comply with a political policy that she finds suboptimal, perhaps foolish, erroneous, or even bad. She knows that if she does not comply, she renders herself liable to the coercive force of the governing body, perhaps in the form of punishment. You will recall the fundamental question democratic theory tries to respond to: How can force of this kind be rendered consistent with Frances's status as an equal? Isn't Frances simply being bossed around by her fellow citizens, who happen to form a majority?

The deliberative democrat claims that the reason why Frances is required to comply with the outcome she opposes is that, prior to voting, all citizens had the opportunity to exchange not merely their opinions and preferences, but their reasons in support of their views. As it turns out, Frances and her allies did not manage to persuade enough people of the force of the reasons that support her favored outcome. The deliberative democratic process, then, is held to respect Frances's equality in virtue of the fact that it gives the reasons she endorses—reasons both in favor of her own view and against opposing views—a hearing. More important than this, it enables Frances to access the reasons of her fellow citizens, the considerations that lead them to favor a view different from her own. So, the thought runs, even though she must now comply with a result she opposes, Frances can see, and perhaps even in some sense appreciate, the reasons that support that result. Moreover she can see how her fellow citizens were led to adopt their view. She can also see how she should move forward in criticizing the result and pressing for its reform; in addition to opposing the outcome, she can contest the reasoning and the reasons that are alleged to support it.[11] In a nutshell, the deliberative democrat holds that self-government among equals is realized when collective decision-making is driven by processes in which citizens reason together.

Deliberativism is well attuned to the difficulties raised earlier concerning inequalities in social standing. It holds, in effect, that the democratic ideal is not realized unless all citizens' reasons are given a fair hearing in a social process of public deliberation, where individuals are not only willing to question the views of others, but also open to having their own political views challenged (and their minds changed). This goes some distance in showing that democracy requires institutions and policies designed to constrain the ways in which money and other forms of social privilege can be transformed into political power.

Furthermore, by requiring that democratic deliberation be public, deliberativism addresses the concern that the prevalence of bigoted and unjust discriminatory attitudes in the background culture of a democracy will undermine equality. For one thing, the deliberativists insists that public deliberation must be inclusive of the public. Thus, informal blocks to citizens' access to processes of democratic reasoning must be eliminated. Moreover, the need for deliberation to be public also helps root out and neutralize political views that derive from racism, sexism, and other forms of unjust discrimination. When addressing and evaluating each other's *reasons*, certain kinds of considerations are rendered irrelevant, or even inadmissible; expressions of bigoted attitudes, no matter how popular, do not serve as reasons, and so cannot provide grounds for a democratic outcome. Drawing these together, we can say that on the deliberative view, political reasoning must be public in at least two senses: first, it must be conducted in spaces that make available to citizens opportunities to participate; second, it must be conducted by reasons that are themselves nonexclusionary and generally accessible to citizens as such.

Deliberative democracy, at least in the broad construal that has been described, is the predominant framework among contemporary democratic theorists. Consequently, there are many distinct varieties of deliberative democratic theory in currency, and a lot more would need to be said in order to flesh out any particular version of the view. Moreover, deliberativism faces several internal difficulties, and thus deliberative democrats of varying stripes engage in internecine debates over, say, the nature of "generally accessible reasons," and the like. But we need not address these matters. Our purposes lie elsewhere. To wit, recall the vocabulary introduced earlier of the *scope, site,* and *reach* of democracy. Our discussion thus far has been aimed at demonstrating that theoretical attempts to capture the democratic ideal lead to expanding conceptions of democracy's reach.

To see this, consider first the expansion of democracy's scope that deliberative democracy invokes. According to the deliberative democrat, democratic citizens owe each other justifications—in the form of generally accessible and publicly stated reasons—for their political positions. The readiness and capacity to publicly exchange political reasons is taken to be a hallmark of the kind of *respect* that citizens must show toward one another.[12] Hence, according to most deliberative views, the scope of democracy includes a general requirement for citizens to discuss and deliberate together, to engage each other's reasons, concerns, criticisms, and perspectives, to gather information, to pay attention to the political issues of the day, and so on. Voting or politically advocating simply on the basis of one's preferences is regarded as an irresponsible, perhaps blameworthy, exercise of the powers of citizenship. Moreover, the deliberative model involves a stronger duty on the part of elected officials and policymakers to communicate the reasons driving public policies, to make the case to the public for whatever is done in their name, and to stand prepared to respond to criticisms and questions concerning the official rationales offered.

This expansion of democracy's scope naturally involves a corresponding enlargement of its site. The deliberative model holds that all social spaces are at least presumptive venues for the exercise of democratic citizenship. According to the deliberativist, any place in which citizens can discuss politics is by default within the site of democracy. Recognizing that some spaces where citizens may discuss politics are structurally unsuited to proper deliberation, many deliberative democrats call for the creation of new venues explicitly designated for deliberative activity. The idea is that, as democracy requires widespread public engagement in the form of political deliberation among citizens, the site of democracy must be expanded so as to allow for widespread access and exposure to well-structured democratic activity. Consequently, the deliberativist includes among democracy's site physical spaces such as parks, sidewalks and street corners, public buildings, coffee shops, and campuses as well as the nonphysical space of the media environment and the Internet.

On the deliberativist view, then, politics quickly becomes, at least presumptively, omnipresent. Now, I suppose that theorists of deliberative democracy are prepared to place certain kinds of social venues—perhaps family holiday dinners and similar gatherings among intimates—presumptively outside the site of democratic politics. As I suggested earlier, there are certain social contexts where political discussion is *out of place* due to the fact that, within the context, the prevailing bonds of interpersonal relationships prevent persons from holding each other accountable as citizens. It is telling, however, that although in the vast and still expanding literature on deliberative democracy a great deal of attention is paid to difficulties concerning the transformation of social spaces into properly deliberative ones, almost no attention has been paid to the question of where and when political deliberation should be unwelcome.

In short, on most deliberative views the entire social sphere is placed within the reach of democratic politics by default. That is, deliberativists tend to see the whole of social space as, at least presumptively, a potential arena for politics, and they regard nearly everything we do as a possible exercise of democratic citizenship. We can say, then, that deliberativism involves a *maximalist* interpretation of democracy's reach. It recommends as extensive an interpretation of the scope and site of democracy as can be plausibly envisioned. Moreover, it prescribes the extension of democracy's reach into any venue where citizens could be expected to exchange ideas about politics, and it then prescribes a vision of democracy according to which citizens are perpetually talking politics. It says that democratic citizenship could be exercised almost anywhere, and probably should be.

2.5 Expanded Democracy in Practice

For those who feel the grip of the moral problem to which democracy is addressed, deliberative democracy is a promising response. I should add that, in my view, some version of deliberativism is correct; I hold that a certain version of deliberative democracy in fact succeeds as reconciling the state's entitlement to coercive power with the fundamental moral equality of democratic citizens. However, the point of the preceding discussion has not been to assess or recommend the theory of deliberative democracy. Rather, I have tried to show that an intuitive way of thinking about democracy leads us to see it as a social ideal, and this in turn inevitably draws us toward increasingly expansive conceptions of democracy's reach. Deliberative democracy is the culmination of this tendency, as it embraces a maximalist conception of the reach of democratic politics. Again, it is important to observe that this trend of expanding the reach of politics emerges from within the idea of democracy itself.

Although the discussion thus far has been focused on the trajectory of contemporary democratic theory, the phenomena we have been tracing are not merely theoretical. Return to the rough sketch of our workaday conception of democracy with which this chapter began. The description of democracy offered by the deliberativist matches what we commonly *take ourselves to be doing* when we engage in political activity. From the perspective of our political self-conception, we're all deliberative democrats.

That claim calls for clarification. It is obvious that current democratic practice falls far short of the ideal envisioned by the deliberativist. For one thing, current modes of democratic practice fail to track citizens' public reasons and do not manifest a sufficient degree of inclusive and respectful deliberation among citizens. And no deliberative democrat embraces the political status quo in contemporary democracies.

Nonetheless, we are all deliberative democrats in the sense that political practice *aspires* to deliberative democracy. No matter how far short we may fall, deliberative democracy is what we are trying to do, and, more importantly for present purposes, it is most often what we see ourselves as doing when we engage politically. As was noted at the start of this chapter, citizens embrace a conception of democracy according to which talking, arguing, speaking out, and answering criticisms is the name of the game; accordingly they take reasons to be the central currency of democratic politics. Likewise, they tend to endorse the idea that democratic citizens have a duty to be informed, to discuss and argue, to hear the reasons of their political opponents, and to try to address challenges and objections to their views. They think that citizens should endeavor to grasp the reasons and arguments driving the central policy debates of the day. They strive to base their political views on reasons and arguments. They take themselves to have a better grasp of the relevant facts and reasons than their opponents do. They expect officials and office holders to be articulate reason-givers, and criticize them harshly when they seem unable to meet objections, answer questions, and formulate objections to alternative views. What's more, large numbers of citizens devour the books, columns, podcasts, and television programming devoted to political debate. And they instinctively think that others who engage politically strictly on the basis of habit, tradition, instinct, or unreflective preference are thereby worthy of criticism.

Furthermore, popular critiques of existing democratic politics tend to invoke the deliberative ideals. Politicians, pundits, and citizens from across the spectrum of opinion frequently lament the inability to respectfully disagree, as well as the general intransigence, that pervade contemporary politics. Citizens readily diagnose persistent political disagreement in ways that impugn the deliberative practices and rational capacities of their opponents; they attribute to those politically on the other side various degrees of ignorance, pigheadedness, irrationality, and benightedness. As we will have

occasion to note later in a slightly different context, terms such as
"spin," "derp," "bias," "flip-flopping," "fake news," "alternative facts,"
"post-truth," and the like are deployed when criticizing others for
failing to respond appropriately to reasons. In short, contemporary
citizens hold their political practices to the deliberative democratic
ideal. They expect citizens, politicians, pundits, and other officials
to engage in civil public deliberation; they demand that political decision and public policy be driven by reasons, rather than by force,
brute preference, insider influence, and money.

Embracing the deliberativist prescriptions for how democratic
politics should get done is of course consistent with failing to do
politics in those ways. And, as was just mentioned, there is an uncommonly widespread consensus across the political spectrum
that contemporary democracies are indeed doing politics badly.
Although democratic citizens are more than ever involved in political discussion, debate, and engagement of a certain sort, current
democratic politics seems plagued by increasing degrees of incivility, deadlock, distrust, hostility, antagonism, and cynicism. The
positive correlation between increased participation in political
activities and political dysfunction is curious, and in the next two
chapters I will offer an explanation of it. But the looming question
is what can be done to repair our politics amidst enhanced public
engagement.

It has seemed obvious to some deliberativists that the problem
lies with the ways in which citizens are enacting the activities of
deliberative democracy. There is plenty of evidence for the view
that although citizens take themselves to be reasoning and arguing
in earnest, they in fact—and often unwittingly—are merely
reinforcing their prejudices, marginalizing their critics, and
assembling silos of like-minded fellow citizens. The mechanism by
which this kind of democratic self-deception occurs is easy to identify. The communications technology that supports such robust
political engagement also enables citizens to construct their own
political media environments that function like echo chambers

where citizens are exposed only to different articulations of their own ideas, and so eventually become less able to manage political disagreement. This phenomenon will be explored fully in coming chapters.

In light of this, some theorists of deliberative democracy have recommended interventions designed to encourage political engagement among diverse citizens and discourage political deliberation among homogeneous groups of citizens.[13] Others have proposed incentives for citizens to participate in properly curated deliberation events.[14] And these recommendations are sometimes accompanied by calls for the establishment of new political institutions designed to facilitate and enhance public deliberation.[15]

Proposals of these kinds will be discussed in Chapter 5. For now, the point is that even if one concedes that such measures are indeed necessary for rehabilitating democratic practice, the argument I am about to launch will suggest that these interventions are bound to backfire unless they are introduced alongside efforts of a different kind. More precisely, any interventions we might introduce for enhancing democratic practice must be accompanied by initiatives aimed at encouraging arenas of cooperative engagement that are nonpolitical, activities that are not already structured around political projects and profiles. To return to the central theme, the deliberative democrats' proposals for rehabilitating democracy can fully succeed only once politics has been put in its place.

2.6 Overdoing Democracy as an Internal Problem

This concludes Part One of this book. In these two preliminary chapters, I first argued that although I am calling for constraining democracy's reach, there's nothing antidemocratic afoot. Holding that we must put politics in its place is consistent with embracing robust conceptions of democracy, democratic citizenship, and political engagement. I then tried to demonstrate that the problem of overdoing democracy emerges from within the democratic ideal itself; it is in the sense an *endemic* or *native* challenge that contemporary democracy must confront.

It is important to appreciate the internal nature of the problem because many of the leading diagnoses of democracy's present ills (and there is a surplus of such diagnoses) locate the problem within some external factor that has infiltrated the political sphere and distorted democracy. Market-thinking and related norms of "individualism" are commonly cast in the role of the invading force, and consequently the prescription for democracy's dysfunction is always some version of the Addams and Dewey elixir, *more democracy*. But I have suggested in the foregoing that it might be rather that democracy's ills, including possibly the infiltration of nondemocratic norms from the business world into the sphere of politics, are due to internal forces within the democratic ideal itself. I will try in the coming chapters to make the full case for this view. But it should be emphasized once again that if I am correct, if our political troubles are the result of overdoing democracy, then the prescription offered by the competing analyses are not only misplaced and unlikely to succeed; they also could be positively counterproductive. In other words, if the problem is overdoing democracy, and the solution is to put politics in its place, then responding by doing more democracy straightforwardly exacerbates the problem—our redoubled efforts to enact proper democracy are destined to backfire in the absence of initiatives of a fundamentally different kind. I fear that, as things stand, democracy's troubles are now severe enough that we cannot afford to aggravate them any further.

With the thesis clarified and the ground cleared, it remains to make the case.

PART II
DIAGNOSIS

3

The Political Saturation
of Social Space

The case for the core thesis of this book proceeds by way of two distinct arguments—one diagnostic, the other prescriptive. The diagnostic argument aims to establish that, in the United States and elsewhere, democracy needs to be put in its place if it is to thrive. The diagnostic argument will be presented in this chapter and the next. Together, these two chapters identify the mechanisms by which democracy comes to be overdone. The second, prescriptive argument will be developed in Chapter 5 and augmented in Chapter 6. It proposes a strategy for putting politics in its place.

The diagnostic argument relies heavily on data that draw from the United States and, to a lesser extent, the United Kingdom. In the preceding chapters, I sought explicitly to indicate the constrained scope of the empirical claim that democracy is being overdone by adding qualifications like the one I deployed in the previous paragraph, "in the United States and elsewhere." In the remaining chapters, I largely omit such phrases not because I contend that all democracies are overdoing their politics, but rather for the sake of simplicity of expression.

To be sure, there is a question worth pursuing about why the problem of overdoing democracy is so prevalent in the United States. Some have suggested that certain structural features of US democracy—specifically its two-party system and winner-take-all elections—are the central causes of the problem. No doubt these contribute, and surely institutional and constitutional design can help curb democracy's overdoing. Nonetheless, trends similar to the ones discussed in this chapter are to be found in the United Kingdom, and the national divides over Brexit and related matter that one finds there replicate the tendencies that prevail in the United States.[1] What's more, the troubling lurches in the direction of populism and nationalism that have beset many of the continental European democracies manifest political inclinations much like the ones to be discussed here.[2]

The empirical elements of the diagnostic argument nonetheless reflect *trends*, and so naturally there are significant academic debates concerning their durability and robustness. No doubt some will regard the account offered here as dependent on a pessimistic or alarmist interpretation of the extant data. Time—and further research—will tell us more about how to understand these trends. Nonetheless, recall that if the argument from Chapter 2 is correct, the problem of overdoing democracy emerges out of the democratic ideal itself. Thus there is a sense in which no democratic society is fully immune to the problem of overdoing its politics. Those readers who adopt a different understanding of the data, or who are lucky enough to be living in a democracy that is currently not plagued by the phenomena that will be outlined, should regard the account presented here as a cautionary tale about democracy. The question of which existing democracies (if any) fit the description I will provide is different from the question of whether democracy is vulnerable in the ways I will be describing.

3.1 Preview of the Diagnostic Argument

As I have mentioned, the diagnostic argument will be presented in the course of two chapters. The diagnostic argument combines empirical and conceptual points, thus it might be helpful to begin with a succinct sketch of its general contours. With a sense of the overall shape of forest, one can better appreciate the path amidst the trees.

In the United States and other democracies, the past several decades have seen increasing political divisions among citizens, politicians, parties, and political organizations more generally. This development has occurred alongside a broader trend within democratic populations of social *sorting* that tracks political divides. What this means is that social spaces are growing increasingly politically homogeneous. The trend is robust, applying to social spaces across the board, from shopping malls, cafés, restaurants, grocery stores, and movie theaters to households, neighborhoods, workplaces, public parks, and places of worship. Along with this, there has also been a similarly steady sorting of sources of news, information, and entertainment along those same political divides. The result is that casual and day-to-day interactions among citizens tend increasingly to occur only among those who share broadly similar political allegiances. And what's more, the everyday political talk that occurs among citizens—whether they be strangers queuing a coffee shop, neighbors watching a little league game, co-workers lunching in a cafeteria, or siblings attending a family gathering—tends to be evermore politically univocal, occurring among like-minded people who not only inhabit those same spaces, but also have comparable experiences, purchase similar consumer goods, take in the same news programming, and share a broad lifestyle and worldview.

Sorting has been accompanied by the expansion of democracy's reach that was charted in the previous chapter. Thus not only have social spaces become more politically homogeneous; those spaces also have become more widely recognized as sites for enactments of democratic citizenship. Further, more and more behavior is now commonly treated as at once an indicator and an expression of one's political allegiances. These days, political significance is commonly ascribed to behavior of all kinds, everything from buying groceries and rooting for a sports team to residing in a given neighborhood, enjoying a particular style of music, or watching one late-night television program rather than another. That is, our sorted social spaces have been colonized by the categories, allegiances, and divisions of politics. The result of this is evident: although democratic citizens are nearly constantly *communicating* their politics to one another, only very rarely do they occupy spaces that are politically mixed. Hence we are more often than ever enacting the office of citizenship in ways that may seem to satisfy the public engagement models of democratic society, but we do so under conditions that are structurally nondemocratic because, due to sorting, they are socially and politically homogenous. Call this combination of widespread social sorting and the infiltration of the categories and allegiances of politics into all aspects of social life the *political saturation of the social*, or *political saturation* for short.

Political saturation initially might not seem especially problematic. Perhaps it is merely the upshot of the facts that people enjoy the company of like-minded others and also take seriously their duties as democratic citizens. Or maybe sorting represents an exercise of citizens' liberty, and their extension of political categories into all areas of social life expresses their civic responsibility. So where's the problem?

There can be little doubt that political saturation is the natural result of individual choice. However, I am not advancing the claim that in all areas of life citizens intentionally seek to hive together in politically like-minded enclaves so as to eschew interactions with anyone who does not share their own perspective; as philosophers say, they do not act *under that description*. The choices that have resulted in political saturation are driven by the benign desire to feel at home in the world. However, even though our present circumstance permits an innocuous causal explanation of this kind, we nevertheless inhabit politically saturated social spaces, and this bodes poorly for democracy.

The full account of how the political saturation of the social negatively impacts democracy will come in Chapter 4, where I complete the diagnostic argument by examining the widely studied phenomenon of *belief polarization*. This phenomenon supplies good reason to hold that extended political activity under conditions of political saturation erodes certain capacities that are required for proper democratic citizenship. As those capacities dissolve, democratic citizens lose the ability to cultivate some of the social goods that it is the *point* of democracy to secure. More importantly, the nurturing of some of these social goods is *prerequisite* for healthy democratic politics. Thus, to recall the discussion in Chapter 1, political saturation produces a social environment where widespread and robust participation in democratic politics crowds out and eventually dissolves these other social goods. Democracy is thereby smothered, and in its place is left a dysfunctional politics driven by spectacles of animosity, outrage, and distrust from which conscientious citizens cannot look away. But, in their fixation, citizens only escalate the dysfunction. In overdoing democracy, citizens hasten its demise.

That's the general shape of the diagnostic argument. If this diagnosis is correct, the general character of the prescriptive argument to be developed in Chapter 5 is easily discerned. If we are to rehabilitate democracy, we need to constrain its reach so that those other social goods can be cultivated. To revert to a familiar theme, we need to put politics in its place by devising venues in which we sometimes can do things together that are not already saturated with politics. Of course, before any such prescriptions can be proposed, the relevant diagnostic claims about sorting, political saturation, and polarization must be defended. Again, sorting and saturation are addressed in the present chapter; polarization will be discussed in Chapter 4.

Before beginning, some background about sorting must be set in place. The literature regarding social sorting is vast. A popular and influential 2008 book by journalist Bill Bishop (with the political scientist Robert Cushing) titled *The Big Sort* captured the public mind by calling attention to the phenomenon of sorting, which Bishop's subtitle alleges is "tearing us apart." In 2014, the Pew Research Center produced a dense report corroborating many of Bishop's findings. Pew's "Political Polarization in the American Public" opens with the claim that "Republicans and Democrats are more divided along ideological lines—and partisan antipathy is deeper and more extensive—than at any point in the last two decades."[3] The report goes on to document a range of disquieting trends that suggest a thoroughly fractured citizenry not only separated by geography and politics, but opposed in nearly every conceivable way, from consumer habits and entertainment preferences to religious affiliation and fertility rates. In a 2016 follow-up report, Pew's dim findings were reaffirmed; "Americans are increasingly sorted into think-alike communities that reflect not only their politics but their demographics."[4]

Following the publication of Bishop's book, a large number of researchers picked up the theme of concurrent and mutually reinforcing spatial and ideological division among the US population, creating a sizeable and active industry focused on debates over the nature, extent, and causes of the sorting phenomena. As one would expect, some researchers find in the most current data confirmation of the views presented by Bishop and Pew, whereas others remain skeptical.[5] I cannot canvass these debates here, though it does strike me (and it has struck others) that a good deal of the controversy is semantic, driven by competing conceptions of the phenomena under investigation and correspondingly divergent views about how they are to be measured.[6] At any rate, there is little academic debate over whether sorting—the spatial and social clustering of citizens into opposing politically partisan groups—is occurring in the United States. The presentation of the sorting data that will be offered here does not deviate from mainstream interpretations in the academic literature. So much for the preliminaries. Once again, we begin from square one.

3.2 Expanding the Local

Let's start with some observations that might seem distant from our topic. When we use the term *technology*, we typically are referring to whatever technology is *new*. These days, it would sound odd to refer to landline telephones or automobiles as *technology*. But it sometimes pays to keep a term's connotations distinct from its meaning. By technology, one need not mean the *latest* innovation or advance; a technology is a technique or intervention developed by humans for the sake of facilitating some objective.

Keeping this in mind, note that most technology simultaneously enlarges and shrinks the world. Although that may initially sound paradoxical, it really isn't. To take a simple example, think about the commonplace technology of air travel. This includes the vast and coordinated network of planes, airports, air traffic controls, weather monitoring, communications platforms, pilots, attendants, baggage handlers, and so on. It all seems unremarkable to us now, which is why we often do not think of air travel as an example of technology at all. However, with nearly ninety thousand domestic flights occurring each day in the United States alone, the system truly is a technological marvel. And, like most technology, it has transformed our lives. Widespread access to affordable and safe flights has changed everything from business, commerce, and trade to research, education, and leisure. To be more specific, in all of these areas, air travel has shrunk the distance between people and places. It thereby has expanded each individual's network of relationships, activities, responsibilities, and experiences.

For instance, my job has me regularly travelling on planes to places far from my home in Nashville, Tennessee, to conduct and share research with colleagues who otherwise I probably would never have met. And, judging from the casual chatter that occurs among passengers on some of my flights, it's common for people in other occupations to commute by airplane for job-related activities. It is not too far of a stretch to say that, for many of these commuters, their workplace encompasses several geographically disparate cities, and their co-workers are individuals who live all across the globe.

So it is with technological innovations more generally. They tend to shrink the world by enabling individuals to access larger portions of it more easily. In this sense the world is simultaneously enlarged and shrunk. To put the point figuratively, technology tends to *expand the local*.

That is not all. As the local is expanded, the power of individual choice is correspondingly augmented. Having access to larger portions of the world around us also extends the range of options we confront when making choices of nearly all kinds. Think again of business passengers on their planes, some of who can be assumed to be commuting by air to the physical space in which they work. Were it not for air travel, they would have had to live much closer to their workplaces, or else taken different jobs. So their options regarding housing, schooling, and many other lifestyle issues would have been far more limited than they in fact are. A similar story can be told about an academic friend of mine for whom the availability of affordable air travel to particular historical sites enabled her to choose as her research focus the issues in her field that she finds the most gripping; without access to those sites, she would have had to specialize in something else. As I type this sentence I can see an international group of prospective students and their parents touring the campus of my university. Were it not for affordable air travel, many of these young adults could never have considered attending Vanderbilt. Or take an example that's closer to home: thanks to overnight air shipping, it is possible to enjoy fresh Maine lobster at a restaurant in the middle of the Nevada desert.

It's a small world, after all. And in growing small, the world also has become *made to order*. This is why technological advances are frequently experienced as empowering, sometimes even liberating. By expanding our access to greater portions of the world, technology provides a richer field of options from which we may choose. It opens new possibilities while at the same time putting us more firmly in charge of our environments. Thus we have become unstuck to the world as it is found; the spaces we inhabit are now thoroughly customizable and hence *personalized*.

That's certainly not technology's full story. Once we turn attention toward the most recent technological developments, the limitations of the previous account become apparent. Some technologies are valuable precisely because they constrain choice by eliminating or hiding options. Algorithm-driven Internet search engines and similar online operations are helpful to us precisely because they filter out certain options. Some argue that these technologies nonetheless empower us by enabling individuals to *choose not to choose*.[7] Yet, at the same time, they direct our choosing by selecting the order and presentation of our options, thereby "nudging" us toward certain selections and away from others.[8] Thus the liberating capacity of modern technology might be largely illusory.[9] In addition to this, we must not overlook the fact that the capacity of most technology to empower individuals is almost always accompanied by features that can facilitate surveillance, manipulation, intrusion, theft, and so on. Hence there is at least a question as to whether current technology empowers us. Perhaps the safest thing to say here is that the character and impact of any technology depends centrally upon who is in control of it.

These larger issues need not be engaged here, however, as our present theme is comparatively pedestrian. Over the past several decades, technological advances—specifically in the areas of travel, commerce, communications, and computing—have enabled large numbers of individuals to enjoy new forms of latitude concerning how they live their lives. Our *lifestyle* is, perhaps more than ever before, up to us. With the expansion of the local that contemporary technologies effect, we are less constrained by the limitations inherent in our immediate environs. Residing in Reno no longer means that one will have to forgo fresh seafood;

someone in Wichita learning Arabic can have real-time, face-to-face conversations with native speakers in Tripoli; a fan of obscure Japanese animated cinema living in Scranton can not only readily access the latest films in the genre, but also can join a global community of fellow enthusiasts; and a successful Hollywood screenwriter can live in New Jersey. For those of us who enjoy unrestricted Internet access, the whole world is at our fingertips. What's more, the parts of the world we inhabit are rendered malleable, subject to our individual wills. To repeat, we live in a made to order world.

3.3 Sorting: Physical, Social, and Political

All of this is largely to the good. However, a substantial body of research indicates that what has emerged from individuals exercising this newfound latitude is a steady pattern of segregation—*sorting*—by which demographically similar people come to occupy the same physical and social spaces, to the exclusion of those who are dissimilar from themselves. That is, over the past several decades in the United States, the expansion of the country's overall diversity in race, ethnicity, religion, age, acculturation, and other relevant demographic categories has been accompanied by *increased* homogeneity along these same dimensions in geographic regions within the country.[10] Apart from some of the large metropolises that remain proverbial melting pots, the geography of the United States is now markedly sorted into distinct demographic groups, each with its own ascendant socioeconomic, racial, ethnic, generational, and religious profile.[11] And this same trend of homogenization is evident within households, neighborhoods, municipalities, workplaces, schools, public parks, shopping centers, places of worship, and social networks in general.[12] Put succinctly, contemporary technology has served up made to order worlds, and most people have made the world they inhabit in their own image.

This "birds of a feather" tendency—*homophily*—is hardly surprising. The ancient Greeks affirmed as a basic fact of human sociology that "like favors like."[13] Moreover, the capacity of randomly assembled individuals to spontaneously organize themselves into opposing subgroups on the basis of perceived (even if not exactly real) similarity and difference is well documented and remarkably durable.[14] We need not explore the question of what psychological mechanisms drive homophily; our concern lies simply with the fact that the trend is widespread.

Like favors like. The corresponding tendency toward sorting thus appears unremarkable when considered in isolation from its broader social context. So let's now consider this context. First note that as physical and social spaces become more demographically homogeneous, the behavioral patterns of those who inhabit them also grow alike. Distinct regions of the United States now have increasingly disparate marriage and fertility rates; and conceptions of community, family, and even childrearing have become markedly regionalized.[15] Moreover, casual consumption habits, leisure activities, pastimes, as well as more intimate matters are now tightly tied to geography. So much so that the software company Esri has established a website called Tapestry where one can enter a US zip code and receive in return a succinct but detailed—and often stunningly accurate—breakdown of the median age, spending habits, family size, living arrangements, values, and even hobbies of the people who live there.[16] Another Internet service named Teleport draws upon the trend from the other side of the equation; it advises users on cities to consider moving to, based on information they provide about economic circumstance and lifestyle preferences. The Teleport web page describes the program as one that will "move you to the best place to live and work" all "based on your personal preferences"; the site also offers relocation services.[17] As one journalist puts it, "Your zip code is a window into what you can afford to buy, but it also reveals how you spend time—and, in essence, *who you are*."[18]

Again, given the unprecedented latitude that individuals now enjoy, this is unsurprising. But next consider explicitly what has been lurking in the background all along: sorting tracks our *political* profiles. The resulting clusters of individuals in homogeneous physical and social spaces reflect their political divisions.[19] As a consequence, demographically and geographically sorted social spaces are also sites of political like-mindedness.

This phenomenon is perhaps most evident in American churches. Whereas it once had been common for congregations intentionally to adopt a resolutely apolitical stance, it is now uncommon to find a religious community in the United States that does not explicitly itself with some affiliation along the political spectrum of "liberal" and "conservative." It is similarly common to find pastors and preachers overtly endorsing political candidates, parties, and policies. Importantly, a standard account of this transformation has it that across the country, the leadership of the various denominations came to be politicized, and so began injecting politics into their services and identities. However, there is reason to think that this account gets things backwards—the politicization of American churches is a *product* of the broader trend by which citizens find their identity in their political affiliation.[20] The congregants' identification with a political lifestyle has driven the pastors to inject political messaging into their services.

The ramifications extend rapidly. Families, civic organizations, and social clubs have grown strikingly more politically univocal over the past thirty years. Traditional, politically mixed voluntary civic associations—veterans groups, fraternal orders, public service clubs, and the like—have withered and been replaced by professionally managed and partisan-specific political advocacy organizations.[21] Workplaces, which not long ago were notable sites of cooperative activity among politically dissimilar citizens, are now largely politically segmented.[22] Moreover, job candidates who are believed to share the dominant political affiliation of a firm are favored in hiring decisions.[23] And certain professions—banking, technology, education, law, and medicine—now skew decidedly along partisan lines.[24]

More than this, political profiles have come to be dramatically reliable markers of individuals' broader lifestyle proclivities. To cite one surprising example, liberals and conservatives predictably decorate their homes and workspaces in systematically different ways—conservative spaces feature more clocks and less art than those occupied by liberals.[25] A more momentous illustration lies in the fact that political affiliation has become a "litmus test for interpersonal relations" of nearly every kind.[26] This includes relations associated not only with friendship and neighborliness, but also with the more intimate matters of romance and even marriage. Data suggest that aversion to politically mixed marriage has increased over the past two decades and is intensifying within some populations.[27] Research also has found that "marital selection based on partisanship exceeds selection based on physical (e.g., body shape) and personality attributes."[28] Coupling patterns within online dating communities reveal similar trends. Importantly, these studies of coupling trends show that co-partisanship is the mechanism driving the interpersonal affinity; the experiments correct for the possibility that romantic attraction might be tracking some nonpolitical feature of persons that happens to correlate with partisan affiliation.[29] Some studies even have found a correlation between partisan identity and membership on websites that facilitate adulterous encounters.[30]

Apart from romantic coupling, judgments of the attractiveness of faces track partisan cues. Even when the identifying signals are subtle, we tend to find political co-partisans more attractive than those with political commitments that differ from our own.[31] Consequently the folk wisdom within the online dating community is to refrain from including mention of one's political commitments on one's public profile; this tends to increase one's options. In any case, according to recent data, "Political ideology is the strongest predictor of successful online matchmaking."[32]

In a nutshell, the trends aligning political profile with broader social identities and lifestyle are strikingly robust. As Bishop puts it, "Choosing to be a Republican or a Democrat [reflects] a way of life."[33] Lilliana Mason and Julie Wronski express a similar conclusion more elegantly—"All politics is identity politics."[34] It's no stretch to say that today politics *simply is* our lifestyle.[35]

In modern democracies, lifestyle is tightly bound to patterns of consumption.[36] Try this experiment: Take a moment to visit an online comments thread where opposed partisans flame each other, and note how quickly and often political argument is presented alongside criticism of what is perceived to be the opposition's purchasing behavior: "latte-drinking snowflake," "pickup-driving hillbilly," and "Walmart shopper" and the like are strikingly common terms of abuse.

Given this, it should not be surprising that *commercial spaces* have also become more socially sorted and hence more politically homogeneous. As is commonly observed in popular media, Walmart and Target serve politically distinct clientele, as do Dunkin' Donuts and Starbucks, as well as Chick-fil-A and Chipotle.[37] Not incidentally, commercial marketing is now explicitly designed to target customers based on their political identities. To cite just one illustration, by repurposing foreign words to serve as the name of its drinks and decorating their stores with maps and photos of remote places, Starbucks overtly aims to appeal to the cosmopolitan self-image of the broadly liberal demographic it seeks to serve. By contrast, Dunkin' Donuts strives to associate coffee and doughnuts with the patriotic value of hard work ("America Runs on Dunkin'" is the current slogan), thereby aiming to capture conservative customers who want inexpensive caffeine and carbohydrates rather than the momentary semblance of being in a foreign country. Similar explanations can be given of the marketing of almost anything. Advertising for cars and trucks, beer, clothing, chain restaurants, and grocery stores all manifest this same tendency. Products are marketed by way of appeal to a general lifestyle that is favored by a targeted consumer group; and these lifestyles are now fused tightly with political identity.

And this strategy for attracting customers is effective. Consumer behavior indeed reliably correlates with political allegiances.[38] For example, a study following the 2008 US presidential election found that nearly 90% of the Whole Foods stores in the country are located in counties that Barack Obama carried handily, while just over 60% of the Cracker Barrel restaurants exist in places won by John McCain. This conjunction of political identity and consumer identity is of course a boon to commercial producers and political campaigns alike, as both are now aptly characterized as engaged primarily in branding and marketing.[39] The result is that it is increasingly likely that the person queuing behind you at the grocery store you frequent, or sitting next to you at your local bar, is politically much like you.

The focus thus far has been on the sorting of our physical spaces. But it almost goes without saying that these same patterns are found in the *virtual* spaces we inhabit, including of course the media environments assembled by large-scale news and entertainment organizations. The political impact of 24-hour cable news channels and online newspapers has been examined extensively elsewhere; I need not rehearse these matters here.[40] It suffices to observe that, in keeping with the account presented thus far about the capacity of technology to empower individual choice, citizens now confront personalized news and information environments. And, again in keeping with the tendency of individuals to favor those who they perceive to be like themselves, citizens tend to customize their news intake and other sources of political information so that they align with their antecedent political allegiances.[41]

It is widely lamented that the Fox News Channel and MSNBC serve two distinct populations of US citizen, sorted into "conservatives" and "liberals" respectively. Indeed, these contrasting political profiles are overtly embedded within the two channels' identities. Both feature prime-time programming devoted to political commentary that is expressly allied with either a conservative (Fox) or liberal (MSNBC) perspective.[42] Unsurprisingly, research suggests that the ideological bent of these programs affects the *content* that is reported, which in turn results in significant differences in belief and perception among the different audiences, even with respect to factual matters.[43] A recent Pew study on media consumption among partisans opens with the arresting claim that "when it comes to getting news about politics and government, liberals and conservatives inhabit different worlds."[44]

These trends with respect to political information are obviously further reinforced in broader social media environments, where individual choices exert even greater direct control in the form of "follows," "likes," "retweets," "blocks," and targeted acts of "unfriending." To employ some of the evocative imagery popularized by Cass Sunstein, social media platforms have enabled individuals to construct "echo chambers" and "information cocoons" that allow citizens to insulate themselves from ideas and information that run counter to, or even merely are different from, their own perspectives.[45] And, as Sunstein notes, social media platforms are commonly used in precisely this way, namely as informational sorting devices.[46]

The political impact of these informational silos will be explored in the next chapter; for now, the result is simply that, just like the physical and social spaces that we inhabit, our informational and communicative environments are increasingly the constructions of our choices. And across the board we tend to choose to make these environments in our own images, structured according to the principle of "like favors like." Again, this means that the environments we inhabit—physical, social, and virtual—are increasingly politically homogeneous.

Before moving on, one further dimension of sorting must be emphasized. As a matter of logic, "like favors like" implies no attitudes in particular with respect to those who are unlike. In favoring those who are like oneself, one might be ambivalent toward or wholly uninterested in those who are dissimilar. When it comes to sorting, however, "like favors like" indeed conjoins with the distinct principle that "unlike disfavors unlike." We not only seek company with those who share our broad lifestyle and thus our politics, we also pursue distance from those who are unlike ourselves. In other words, we want not only to be in the company of people who are like ourselves, we want also to be out of the company of those who are different.

Further, sorting has been accompanied by intensifying *animosity* toward one's political opposition. Whereas conservative citizens traditionally could be counted on to report opposition towards the Democratic Party and its leaders (and liberals would similarly report similar attitudes toward the Republican Party and its leaders), they are now disposed to claim that the opposing party makes them fearful and angry.[47] More troubling than this is that animus against one's political opposition is now targeted also toward ordinary "rank and file" citizens who affiliate with the opposed party.[48] We do not merely distance ourselves from those whose politics differ from our own; increasingly, we positively dislike them.

Hence partisans tend to attribute negative traits—including dishonesty, lack of patriotism, incivility, laziness, and untrustworthiness—to citizens on the other side of the divide (while attributing the correlate positive traits to their co-partisans).[49] Moreover, partisans tend to be forgiving of co-partisans for political offenses—stealing campaign signs from yards, for example—that they regard as inexcusable when committed by members of the political opposition.[50] One influential study found that prejudice against affiliates of the opposing party is more severe than bias based in differences of race and religion.[51] And the 2014 Pew report discussed earlier finds that large numbers of citizens are disposed to think that the ideas of the opposing party are not merely misguided or suboptimal, but a "threat to the nation's well-being."[52]

The upshot is clear. The pervasiveness of sorting means that the familiar political divisions and hostilities between Red and Blue, conservative and liberal, Left and Right, are part of the underlying structure of our social environments, segregating our casual and everyday interactions in ways that are not always easily perceived but are nonetheless present and effectual. From the coffee shop and grocery store to the office, church, neighborhood, living room, comments thread, and social media feed, interpersonal interactions are increasingly likely to involve individuals who share a broad political outlook. Relatedly, those same social spaces are increasingly unlikely to bring individuals into face-to-face encounters with anyone who does not share their profile. The political segmenting of the citizenry has been accompanied by escalating antipathy, even animosity, among those on different sides of the divide. As things stand, then, politics has become one's identity, and one's identity is manifest in one's lifestyle; sorting results in a thoroughgoing division of the democratic citizenry into distinct political bodies, living largely different kinds of lives and disinclined to see merit in the lives of those on the other side.

3.4 The Infiltration of Politics

Perhaps it is obvious that sorting poses a serious challenge for democracy. But let's not be too hasty in drawing that conclusion. Pause for a moment to consider an alternative take on the material presented thus far.

One could argue that although the portrait developed in the preceding section is lamentable, there is nothing in it that is *objectionable* from a democratic point of view. A position of this kind might proceed in the following way. As like favors like, it should be expected that exercises of individual latitude would result in socially sorted and politically segmented environments. The accompanying political animosity is but a regrettable byproduct of

the fact that politics often takes the form of a high-stakes competition. Division and distrust among political factions is the inevitable result of democracy. Indeed, given that partisan hostility is
especially intense and seems to be escalating, widespread sorting
should be regarded as a kind of blessing. The sorting of the population into distinct clans, each with its own spaces and lifestyles,
might make for a sturdy balance of political power, which is surely
preferable to what appears to be the most likely alternative, namely
civil war.[53]

Now, whatever the theoretical merits this position may be, the
envisioned power balance, insofar as it exists, is not likely to be
sturdy. This is because the trends I have been documenting contain a *degenerative* element, a component that does not allow for
an enduring truce among political opponents. The full argument
for this claim will come in the next chapter, but to begin to get a
sense of how it will unfold, recall the discussion from the previous
chapter. The ideal of self-government among equals favors a vision
of democratic citizenship as social engagement across a broad ex-
panse of spaces and activities. In a rare convergence of theory and
practice, our democratic activity has in fact travelled this path—we
embrace and enact a maximalist conception of democracy's reach.
So not only do we inhabit sorted and therefore politically homogeneous environments; additionally, our activities are increasingly
regarded as enactments of citizenship. In other words, our social
environments are not merely sorted; they have also been infiltrated
by politics. Sorting has wrought the convergence of politics with
our broader identities, and so our partisan identities spill over into
facets of day-to-day life that otherwise would be regarded as nonpolitical.[54] This in turn has dissolved the boundary between our
everyday behaviors and our political activities, our actions qua citizens. As one group of researchers finds,

Political orientation appears to pervade every aspect of our
public and private lives ... Not only does it describe how we think

about and what we value in terms of government and society as a whole, but it also appears to leave its mark on how we behave towards others, travel, decorate our walls, clean our bodies and our homes, and how we choose to spend our free time.[55]

In the estimation of a different research group, we have entered an era of "lifestyle politics," which is marked by the "tendency to see political meaning in recreational experiences, entertainment choices, fashion decisions, and other personal happenings."[56] In a nutshell, as our political identities have become *who we are*, politics has become *everything that we do*.

As discussed earlier, our characteristic consumption, shopping, leisure, and other activities have become highly reliable indicators of our political allegiances. Recall that, given sorting, conservatives and liberals live systematically different lives; they not only live in different spaces and hold different beliefs, they also drink different beer, drive different cars, follow different sports teams, read different newspapers, eat different kinds of food, and so on.[57] The infiltration of politics adds another dimension to this convergence of politics and lifestyle. Now that nearly everything we do is regarded as political behavior, those same characteristic activities also now serve as *expressions* of our political allegiances, signals to others of where we stand politically.[58]

The convergence of politics and commerce—sometimes discussed in the literature as "political consumerism"—once again provides helpful examples of this expressive aspect of political saturation.[59] Of course, boycotts and "buycotts" are familiar instances where refusing to buy (or buying) is posed as a political act, an expression of one's political allegiances. There is no doubt that collective endeavors of these kinds are vital modes of democratic activity.[60] But let's consider some more recent phenomena in which the infusion of political significance may be more subtle and perhaps more ambivalent.

In my city, tote bags are ubiquitous, and that's surely a good thing. However, totes do not only provide shoppers with a reusable alternative to disposable bags; it is now nearly impossible to find a tote bag that does not display either an advertisement or some message of social conscience (frequently both). Using the tote, like shopping at the market where it was acquired, is as much a way of *signaling* one's political identity to others as it is a way of acting in accordance with one's political values; carrying the tote makes a social statement about one's political allegiances.[61] Just this afternoon I encountered at lunch someone carrying a tote with a clearly visible MSNBC logo accompanied by the message "talk politics to me." This invitation expresses the view that enacting democratic citizenship is appropriate anywhere, but notice that the tote also clearly indicates the political perspective that the person carrying it is likely to espouse. Those who are looking for a reaffirming political discussion are thereby welcomed; others are likely to be deterred. It is worth noting in this connection that although the right-wing websites Breitbart News and Infowars both feature online stores that sell an array of items bearing their logos, including T-shirts, belt buckles, mugs, and flasks, neither sells tote bags.[62]

Camouflage apparel is also ubiquitous where I live, though not in the same areas that one finds the totes. Importantly, these articles of clothing are obviously *not* designed for tactical operations in jungles or deserts; they are most frequently ordinary T-shirts with a camouflage design, often incorporating also a large American flag and an overtly political message. In most cases, the message is recognizably conservative. Just like the MSNBC tote, these shirts are purchased as a way of supporting a political position, and worn publicly as a way of expressing to others a political loyalty that invites some interactions and discourages others. In both cases, the expressive function of the product partly consists in reinforcing the sorting of the social spaces.

Naturally, technology has caught up with the trend of aligning one's consumer behavior with one's politics. A swarm of smartphone apps with names like BuyPartisan, BuyEthical!, and DoneGood enable shoppers to scan the barcode of any product and receive, almost instantaneously, a report of the producer's political allegiances, campaign contributions, trade practices, global investments, and labor policies. The descriptions of these apps often appeal overtly to the politically *communicative* function of shopping, imploring would-be adopters that they should "shop [their] values" and align their spending behavior with their political profiles.

Although I have focused on the intermingling of political identity signaling with consumer behavior in particular, this is not the only site where one can find this aspect of political saturation. It is no exaggeration to say that your everyday choices about the most prosaic and seemingly nonpolitical matters—what television shows to watch, what radio station to listen to, what sports team to follow, what restaurant to frequent, how to get to work, where to vacation, how to spend Sunday mornings, what websites to frequent, and which links to click—are all deeply fused with your political identity in the ways already discussed. And, again, these choices are not only highly correlated with your politics, but also are often ways of publicly expressing your political commitments.

These expressions of your political allegiances in turn serve to further entrench the political homogeneity of your environment. This means that your day-to-day interactions with others are increasingly limited to those who happen also shop at those stores, watch that program, follow that team, take that bus, walk in that park, or comment on that discussion thread, and these others are progressively likely to share your political profile. In short, our social experience is organized around the categories, loyalties, struggles, and animosities of contemporary politics in ways that segregates us—not merely spatially, but ideologically and affectively—from those who are not like ourselves. And, for reasons that will be examined in the next chapter, as our political rivals become more distant and thus more *alien* to us, it becomes increasingly difficult to regard them as our political equals.

3.5 Political Saturation

Thus far I have been describing the interplay of two widespread social forces, namely sorting and the infiltration of politics into the whole of our social environments. The convergence of these two trends results in the *saturation* of our social spaces by politics. As will be argued in the next chapter, political saturation produces the conditions under which democracy is overdone and thus destabilized.

To be clear, I have not been preparing an argument against intensive political activity of the kind that enlists broad behavioral patterns involving consumer and lifestyle choices. Social and political movements great and small require ideologically homogeneous spaces in order to coalesce, foment, organize, and act. The present chapter has not been a prelude to the claim that our political activities must be socially disbursed or else muted. Recall the discussion from Chapter 1: the proper response to overdoing democracy is to do more together that is not politics. This is importantly distinct from the resigning claim (which I reject) that when we engage in political activity, we must do less. In any case, as announced at the start of this chapter, our aim at present is to diagnose the problem of overdoing democracy. By way of conclusion, the dual threads of the foregoing discussion must be more tightly pulled together.

The problem of overdoing democracy surfaces with political saturation, which is the *convergence* of widespread sorting and the infiltration of politics into all aspects of social life. To put the point starkly, as our social environments have been colonized by the categories and allegiances of our politics, we act in the office of citizen more frequently than ever before. Yet, thanks to sorting, those activities are almost never engaged in the politically heterogeneous spaces that are characteristic of a properly functioning democratic polity. As will be argued in the next chapter, when politics saturates the social in this way, our democratic exertions serve to dissolve the conditions that democracy needs in order to flourish. Thus, a variation on a recurring slogan: in overdoing democracy, we undermine it.

Recall once again the argument of Chapter 2. In order to pursue the ideal of self-government among equals, a democracy must strive to be a society in which citizens listen to one another's concerns, examine each other's ideas, and engage together in inclusive and accessible collective reasoning; in short, we must make ourselves *vulnerable* to our fellow citizens' arguments, ideas, and experiences. Only under conditions approximating these can we plausibly see democratic political rule as consistent with each citizens' status as an equal, and thus more than merely the tyranny of the majority. Note, crucially, that this vision of democratic society tacitly presupposes that citizen interactions will occur in politically heterogeneous social environments. The political saturation of social space means that venues of this kind are in rapidly diminishing supply.

That such spaces are becoming ever more rare means that we presently are falling short of the democratic ideal. Now, that we are falling short of such a grand ideal is to be expected. It is the nature of ideals to be aspirational, and, as is commonly affirmed by democratic theorists, democracy is an aspiration that can be more or less fully approximated, but never achieved. The problem, then, is that political saturation results in a politics that falls short in a way that makes for a progressively *dysfunctional* democracy, a democracy that is destined to progressively fall further from the ideal. In order to see this grim implication, an additional diagnostic tool must be introduced into the account—a phenomenon called belief polarization. This is the topic of the next chapter.

4

The Problem of Polarization

Here's a familiar assessment of the present condition of democracy in the United States: politics is more divisive than ever, and severe political divisions are undermining democracy. Ironically, that's the one thing upon which everybody seems to agree. Lamentations over our political divides are commonly accompanied by related warnings concerning political "bubbles," "silos," and "echo chambers"; these are said to produce "intellectual closure," "groupthink," "spin," "derp," "post-truth," and forms of "derangement." All in all, these phenomena result in *polarization*, a condition where political officials and others are so deeply divided that there is no basis for compromise, coordination, or even productive communication. Polarization paralyzes democracy. But in order to thrive, a democracy needs to get things done.

Yet polarization extends beyond the formal apparatus of political parties and public officials. These days, the citizenry is polarized as well. A recent Pew study shows that US citizens are more inclined than ever to regard the ideas of their political opponents as not only misguided, but as a significant threat to the well-being of the nation; they are also more likely to regard citizens who affiliate with an opposition party as unintelligent, dishonest, and immoral.[1] Intriguingly, citizens also report a strong desire for political compromise among governing parties. Alas, there's no silver lining in that result. The Pew study also shows that in this context, US citizens understand "compromise" to mean what one would otherwise call *capitulation*. In other words, they want compromise "on their own terms"; their yearning for compromise is actually a desire for their political opponents to simply give way.[2] Compromise in this sense involves overcoming obstructions rather than meeting others in the middle. Arguably, this is not compromise at all. And so it turns out that citizens' longing for compromise and an easing of partisan division is itself another manifestation of polarization.

The situation seems dire. Unsurprisingly, the genre of popular political writing bustles with warnings about polarization and its dangers.[3] What is less clear in the popular discourse, though, is what is meant by polarization beyond the general condition of intransigence among politicians. Of course, stubbornness among politicians and consequent logjams within government are frustrating, and sometimes even disconcerting. But they are also nothing new. If we are to get a firm grip on what is distinctive about our current political predicament, we need a more precise account of what polarization is. Only then will we be able to discern why it is problematic and how it should be addressed.

The first item on our agenda, then, is to clarify the idea of polarization. I will begin by distinguishing *political polarization* from *belief polarization*. The argument will show that democracy's trouble ultimately lies with the latter, partly because belief polarization is what renders political polarization toxic. This account will in turn help make explicit the ways in which the combination of belief polarization and political saturation render the problem of overdoing democracy *degenerative*, resulting in a condition where our political efforts on behalf of democracy are likely to further democracy's erosion. Thus this chapter completes the diagnostic argument of this book.

4.1 Two Concepts of Polarization: The Rough Distinction

Political polarization and belief polarization are two different ways in which our politics can be characterized as polarized. Let's start with political polarization. It is a measure of the *political distance* between political opponents. As one may expect, there are many ways in which this distance can be understood. One intuitive measure looks to the official platforms of the contending political parties. The degree of political polarization is the extent to which the platforms lack common ground. Alternatively, one might conduct a similar comparison among prominent *politicians* from opposing parties. According to such a view, our democracy is politically polarized to the degree that prominent public representatives of opposing parties share no common policy objectives, plans, or priorities.

These different ways of construing the "distance" that is the mark of political polarization will be discussed more fully later in the chapter. For now, the key point is that political polarization is a relation between political opponents, be they parties or individuals. Thus it is a condition that can exist only when there are opposing political bodies.

Belief polarization, by contrast, occurs *within* a likeminded group.[4] Belief polarization besets individuals who talk only or mainly to others who share their fundamental commitments. To be more specific, when individuals talk mainly with others about the matters upon which they agree, discussants tend gradually to embrace a more extreme version of their initial opinion. This naturally prompts the question of what is meant by *extreme*. Later sections will explore the different ways of understanding the extremity that belief polarization produces. Here note simply that when we talk only to likeminded others, we become polarized not in that we become increasingly distant from our opponents (though that also occurs), but rather in that we come to exchange our initial opinion for one that is more extreme. In short, belief polarization invokes a change in our beliefs; particularly, it involves a change that renders us more extreme versions of ourselves.

There's the rough distinction between political and belief polarization. I acknowledge that this is all still ambiguous, and I assure you that details are coming. Before proceeding, though, recall that it will be argued here that our current political condition is precarious because political polarization has belief polarization at its root. To put the point in a different way, I will be arguing that belief polarization is what renders our political divides especially toxic and progressively debilitating for democracy. So let's turn first to a fuller examination of political polarization.

4.2 Political Polarization

Political polarization is a measure of political division. As previously noted, there are different ways to think about how divisions are to be measured. There are three ways in which political polarization is understood that are relevant here: *platform*, *partisan*, and *affective*.

The first of this trio has already been mentioned. Political polarization can be understood as the *ideological* distance between the *platforms* of competing political parties. When understood in this way, political polarization can occur only within political systems where there are political parties that formulate more or less unified and public platform statements. Where *platform* polarization is acute, competing political parties diverge sharply on nearly every issue. Hence the political middle ground between them dissolves, leaving no basis for cooperation or compromise.

Partisan political polarization, by contrast, is conceptualized as partisan ideological uniformity, what might be aptly characterized as ideological *purity* among partisans. An especially high level of *partisan* political polarization is marked by the absence of moderates within partisan groups, and the gradual weeding out of, say, "conservative Democrats" and "liberal Republicans." One indication of the level of partisan political polarization within the Republican Party at least is the pervasive use of "RINO" (Republican in name only) as a term of derision among party members. As with platform polarization, partisan polarization results in the receding of the middle ground among opposed parties, thus triggering deadlock.

In a third understanding, political polarization is an *affective* distance between political opponents. *Affective* political polarization is marked by high levels within a partisan group of distrust and antipathy toward the members of opposing groups. Note that affective political polarization may prevail among persons who are *not* especially at odds over particular policy issues. What's more, as it is basically a systematic dislike and distrust of one's political opponents, affective polarization might emerge in the absence of significant platform or partisan divisions. Nevertheless, affective polarization results in a breakdown of communication and compromise across partisan divisions, and so, like the other forms of political polarization, it leads to political deadlock.

Although they all result in political deadlock, there are important differences between these understandings of political polarization. For example, as it occurs at the level of party platforms, platform political polarization need not involve any harsh feelings towards one's political opponents. For a different example, notice that partisan political polarization can afflict only those who embrace a systematic collection of political opinions over a range of issues; therefore, it is likely to be found among politicians and party elites rather than ordinary citizens, who tend not to have systematic opinions about political matters. Still, ordinary citizens seem especially susceptible to affective political polarization, as it does not require much by way of ideological consistency or even conviction, but only strong *identification* with a political group. Recall affective polarization is not simply a dislike for those who are different from oneself; it is a dislike of those who one sees as affiliates of an opposing political party.

Is the United States politically polarized? Well, it depends on which kind of political polarization one has in mind. According to many accounts, party elites and members of Congress are far more divided along the partisan and platform dimensions than ordinary citizens are. However, there is general agreement that affective polarization is severe throughout the US citizenry and is growing more intense. In fact, affective political polarization is sometimes understood to be a direct consequence of the sorting phenomena that were examined in the preceding chapter.[5] That sorting, combined with the general political saturation of social space, should result in pervasive and progressing affective political polarization is, perhaps, unsurprising. I will return to the relation among these forces later. What should be noted presently is that these different accounts share a conception of polarization as a condition that exists *between* opposing political bodies that commonly results in political deadlock or stalemate.

4.3 Belief Polarization

Our analysis of belief polarization begins in what may seem to be unlikely places: the sports stadium and concert arena. Take a moment to recall the last time you watched your favorite professional sports team win an important game. Or, if sports aren't your thing, think for a moment of the last time you saw your favorite band perform an especially rousing concert. In attending the game or concert, you immersed yourself in a large group of fellow enthusiasts. Importantly, your immersion was not a matter of simply attending the same event as the other enthusiasts. Rather, in attending the event, you became a kind of *participant* in the group. For example, it is likely that you made an effort to dress like the others by donning a team jersey or a concert shirt; in any case, you sought to signal and express your membership in the group of devotees. And so you unreservedly rooted, applauded, and sang along with the others. In doing these things, you felt swells of excitement, elation, and perhaps even joy. Amidst all the cheering, you probably made some new friends as well. All the while your identification with that team or band was being reinforced. Moreover, in watching the team prevail or the band perform especially well, your mood was elevated. Finally, your estimation of the team members' or performers' talents amplified. In the course of the performance, you came more firmly to hold that the team or band is truly excellent, and thus deserving of your commitment. In this way, the team's victory and the band's exhilarating performance were experienced as an affirmation of your identity as an enthusiast.

I take it that the description captures a familiar phenomenon, the experience of being a *fan*. What is important for our purposes is that when one joins a large group of others to watch a favorite team prevail or a beloved band perform especially well, one experiences a range of satisfying intensifications of mood and affect than in turn affirm one's sense of identity. This in part explains why fandom is so widespread—being a fan generally feels good. More importantly, it also explains why stadiums and music venues are so often crowded; although the benefits that drive us to become fans are largely individual, the rush of being a fan is partly a collective phenomenon— it is enhanced in the presence of other fans. Hence even when we cannot attend the game or performance, we nonetheless devise ways to enjoy it with other fans. Perhaps this collective dimension also helps account for why when a home team loses an important game, the shared frustration and disappointment of the local fans can lead to violence. Fandom is a phenomenon by which we collectively provide to other fans an affirmation of their identity, and so the team's loss can be experienced as a personal affront. Even though there's no "I" in "team," there certainly is a "Me."

There are respects in which belief polarization mirrors the experience of being in a packed stadium surrounded by fellow fans when one's favorite team is winning an important game. As has been said, belief polarization is the tendency whereby discussion among likeminded people results in the participants shifting to a more extreme version of their pre-discussion belief. I'll be arguing that, like fandom, belief polarization involves an intensification of affect that affirms group identity. But the account must be presented with care. Alas, the discussion is about to get a whole lot more *academic*. However, clarifying belief polarization is worth the effort because the phenomenon is not only central to the argument on offer, but is also strikingly widespread.[6]

Let's begin by noting how widespread the phenomenon is. Belief polarization has been found in groups of an extraordinary variety of kinds, from officially defined assemblies—juries, panels of judges, boards of trustees, and investment groups—to informal clusters of ordinary people simply talking about views they share. Moreover, belief polarization does not discriminate between the different *kinds* of belief that group members hold in common. Likeminded groups polarize regardless of whether they are discussing matters of plain fact (such as the elevation of a given city), topics of personal taste (say, the attractiveness of a face or comfortableness of a chair), or questions about value (such as what justice demands in response to a given legal violation).[7] What's more, the phenomenon is found to be active regardless of the explicit *point* of the group's discussion. Likeminded groups polarize when they are talking for the sake of deciding an action that the group will take (e.g., participating in a political protest, rendering a verdict, casting a vote, placing a bet), and they polarize also when there is no specific decision to be reached and no collective action to be taken. Lastly, the phenomenon has been studied throughout the world, and is found to be prevalent in likeminded groups regardless of the demographic profiles of their members; we are vulnerable to belief polarization regardless of nationality, race, gender, religion, economic status, and level of education.

Now for the phenomenon itself. One of the earliest experiments regarding group polarization was conducted in France in the late 1960s with a group of teenage males. The teenagers were asked to discuss both their (variously positive) views about de Gaulle and their (variously negative) views regarding American foreign policy. The individuals emerged with more thoroughly positive views of de Gaulle and more intensely negative views of American foreign policy than those they held prior to the conversation.[8]

In another early study, Michigan high-schoolers were sorted according to their antecedently expressed level of racial prejudice. The likeminded groups then were tasked with discussing several issues regarding race in the United States, including the question of whether racism is the cause of the socioeconomic disadvantages faced by African Americans. Following the conversations with their respective likeminded groups, those who antecedently showed a high level of racial prejudice came to embrace more ardently the view that racism is *not* responsible for the disadvantages faced by African Americans. And those antecedently disposed toward low levels of racial prejudice grew more accepting of the view that racism is indeed the cause of such disadvantages. Once again, discussion among likeminded people amplified the members' pre-discussion tendencies. Moreover, the ideological distance between the two groups expanded.[9]

A similar experiment involved adults who were classified into gender-mixed groups according to their antecedent views concerning the social roles of women. Once sorted into "feminist" and "chauvinist" groups, each group discussed the merits of various statements about the role of women in society—statements like "a woman should be as free as a man to propose marriage," and "women with children should not work outside the home if they don't have to financially." The result was that members of the feminist discussion group became notably more pro-feminist, while the chauvinist group became more chauvinist (though, interestingly, not to a significant degree).[10]

In 2005, a collection of Coloradoans was sorted according to an initial screening into "liberal" and "conservative" groups. Each group was then asked to discuss the following three policy questions:

1. Should states allow same-sex couples to enter into civil unions?
2. Should employers engage in "affirmative action" by giving a preference to members of traditionally disadvantaged groups?

3. Should the United States sign an international treaty to combat global warming?

After discussion within likeminded groups, liberal participants, who were antecedently disposed to favor a global warming treaty, came to endorse more enthusiastically the proposition that the United States should enter into such a treaty. Conservatives who were initially neutral on the idea of such a treaty came to ardently oppose it after discussion with their fellows. Similarly, attitudes towards same-sex civil unions and affirmative action polarized following group discussion in the expected way: liberal support intensified while opposition among conservatives grew more resolute. Importantly, the shift in group members' attitudes also resulted in a greater degree of internal homogeneity. That is, after discussion, not only did the members of each group tend to shift to a view more extreme than the one he or she held prior to the discussion, attitudes within the group also became more uniform. Each shifted into a more extreme version of his or her prior self *and also* became more like the others in the group. Thus belief polarization can contribute to partisan political polarization.[11]

Thus far, I have described experiments demonstrating that discussion in likeminded groups produces shifts in opinion toward extremity in the direction of the individual's pre-discussion inclination. These shifts have been described mainly as intensifications (again, toward extremity in the direction of individuals' initial inclination) of attitude or view. Let's now look at the ways in in which these shifts affect behavior.

Several experiments show that the shifts produced by belief polarization have an effect on individuals' and groups' practical deliberations, and thus their behavior.[12] Consider two cases where this practical ramification of belief polarization is evident. In mock jury experiments involving punitive damage awards, when jury members initially agree that the harm is severe and damages should be awarded, their deliberation produces a verdict of a significantly larger award than any individual juror's initial pre-deliberation assessment. The same goes for juries whose members are initially inclined to think that the harm in question is not particularly extreme and only a low degree of punishment is in order. After deliberation among such jurors, the verdict is more lenient than individual jurors' initial inclination.[13] In both cases, the belief polarization phenomenon results in actions that are more extreme than those individuals would have performed otherwise.

Another study finds that group discussion of an event that participants agree constitutes a serious violation of justice—sex discrimination committed by an elected official, for example— leads to a greater inclination among the discussants to engage in organized protest. But that's not all. Among discussants who see the violation as especially egregious, the enhanced readiness to protest is accompanied by a willingness that exceeds their pre-discussion inclination to protest in ways that are overtly militant (and thus riskier).[14]

In summary, discussion in likeminded groups produces belief polarization. Belief polarization involves a shift toward greater extremity in the beliefs of those subjected to the phenomenon. As one would expect, those shifts tend to manifest behaviors that are more extreme than those that individuals are otherwise disposed to enact. This is what is broadly meant by saying that belief polarization turns us into more extreme versions of ourselves.

It should be acknowledged that the shifts that belief polarization occasions typically occur unconsciously, or at least not deliberately. They are not willful or considered. That is, belief polarization is not a process by which an individual explicitly reasons her way into a more extreme version of herself. By and large, belief polarization *happens to* an individual, often unwittingly.

Such is the basic phenomenon. It would be easy to continue cataloguing experimental findings confirming the tendency. We must not lose sight, however, of the fact that the pervasiveness of belief polarization and the vastness of its documentation only amplify the need for explanation of the *mechanisms* that produce it. Of course, the question of *why* the phenomenon is so pervasive is a matter of ongoing debate. In order to begin to address these matters, we must attend to a few philosophical issues that are already within view.

4.4 Degree, Content, and Commitment

The discussion thus far has involved a certain degree of looseness with concepts at the very core of belief polarization. To put it plainly, the claim that some individual has *shifted to a more extreme version of her initial belief* is ambiguous on multiple fronts.

For starters, one might wonder what is meant by *extreme* in this context. Note first that extremity is understood in a way that makes no reference to a spectrum of opinion. One becomes more extreme in the course of likeminded discussion simply in virtue of moving further in the direction suggested by one's pre-discussion inclination. Accordingly, the shift from finding a particular face "somewhat attractive" to finding it "extremely attractive" is a shift in the direction of extremity as that concept is understood here. Belief polarization consequently need not render one an *extremist* or a *fanatic* in the political senses of those terms (though it might).

Observe also that the concept of extremity being employed invokes no reference to truth. There is no presumption that more extreme beliefs are more likely to be false. Yet, belief polarization typically produces a shift in belief regardless of one's evidence. The phenomenon often causes us to hold beliefs that are not adequately supported by the evidence we have. Thus, insofar as we should believe in proportion to what our evidence warrants, belief polarization indeed worsens our condition. But there is no reason to think that it causes us always to adopt false beliefs.

These points make some progress in clarifying belief polarization. Still, the initial question remains: In what sense of *extreme* does belief polarization render us more extreme? What is involved in "moving further" in the direction of a prior inclination?

The matter is more complicated than it might appear, and the empirical literature is often insufficiently nuanced to address the relevant philosophical issues. Descriptions of the belief polarization experiments often overlook the difference between changes in *degree of belief* and changes in *belief content*. This distinction can be elucidated in the following way. When we hold a belief, we believe *something*. As this is sometimes put, a belief is a kind of affirmative stance we take toward a proposition. So the belief that Nashville is the capital of Tennessee has "Nashville is the capital of Tennessee" as its *content*. But note also then when we hold a belief, we hold it with some degree of confidence. We sometimes say things like, "I *think that* that Nashville is the capital of Tennessee," and "*I'm certain that* Nashville is the capital of Tennessee." Both of these express the same content, but the latter communicates a high degree of belief whereas the former indicates a relatively low degree of belief.[15] We might think of belief content as *what is believed*, and degree of belief as one's *level of confidence* in what is believed.

With this distinction in hand, return to some of the experiments we have discussed. In some, the shift toward extremity might be taken to consist strictly in a boost in the believer's *confidence* in her belief. In the example of the feminists and chauvinists, for instance, the participants seem to hold the same beliefs after the group discussion as the beliefs they held prior to it; they appear to have shifted toward extremity only in the sense that they have come to hold those beliefs *with greater confidence*. Thus the case appears to involve an uptick in *degree* of belief. To be clear, undergoing a significant increase in one's degree of belief is one way in which one might be said to have shifted to extremity, even though it does not involve a change in the content of one's belief.

However, other experiments suggest that the shift involves a change in belief content. Consider the mock jury experiment. In the course of likeminded discussion, the jurors each came to support a different punitive award from the one they advocated prior to their discussion. The Colorado experiment similarly involves a change in content; conservatives started with a neutral view of the proposed global warming treaty, but shifted to a stance of opposition. These are changes in *what is believed*, alterations in the *content* of belief. And, to be clear, the shift from the belief that *the plaintiff deserves a $500 award* to the belief that *the plaintiff deserves a $1,000* award is plausibly regarded as a shift toward extremity.

It is tempting to conclude that there are two different kinds of extremity shift that belief polarization might occasion. One could say that, on the one hand, the phenomenon might produce an extremity shift *of degree*; in the course of likeminded discussion participants intensify the confidence with which they hold the belief they began with. And, on the other hand, belief polarization might prompt an extremity shift in *content*; subjects *replace* their initial belief with one that has a more extreme proposition as its content. On this view, belief polarization is a double-edged phenomenon. It transforms us into more extreme versions of ourselves either by causing us to grow more confident in our pre-discussion belief, or by prompting us to change our pre-discussion belief to some more extreme successor.

However, this tempting conclusion is too tidy to capture the experimental results. Recall that belief polarization involves an increase in *uniformity* among group members. As group members become more extreme versions of themselves, they also become more like one another. This indicates that belief polarization must involve a shift in belief content. Still, the experiments also indicate that belief polarization involves some kind of *intensification*. This raises an important complication. The intensification suggests an uptick in degree of belief; however, in order for an increase in degree of belief to occur, the pre-discussion belief must have the same content as the post-discussion belief. In other words, for an increase in degree of belief to occur, there must be some persisting belief content that subjects come to hold with greater confidence.

However, we have already seen that belief polarization involves changes in belief content. Thus it cannot *also* cause an uptick in degree of belief. Yet surely the mock jury and political protest cases involve *both* a change in belief content *and* some kind of overall escalation of confidence.

Consequently, in order to accommodate the cases in which there is both a shift to more extreme content and some kind of intensification, we must introduce a third feature with respect to which one might become more extreme. In addition to belief content and degree of belief, we can also speak of a believer's level of *commitment to his or her perspective*. That is, we can say that belief polarization occasions the adoption of a successor belief that is more extreme in content than its antecedent, and it also involves an intensification of the believer's commitment to his or her perspective.

Admittedly, in introducing the idea of a *degree of commitment to one's perspective,* I have provoked a swarm of philosophical issues that I cannot address here. My hope is that the motivation for the addition is clear enough: We need to mark the fact that belief polarization intensifies something other than degree of belief. When belief-polarized, we become more ardent devotees of our point of view. So, in the experiments, not only did the pro-feminists shift toward beliefs with more extreme feminist contents, they also became more *ardent feminists*. Similarly, in the experiment about prejudice, not only did those prone to racist prejudice come to adopt more thoroughly prejudiced beliefs, they became *more committed* to their prejudice. And here's why this kind of intensification of commitment is to be expected: it is natural for those who hold more extreme belief contents with regard to some particular issue to also be more fervent devotees of the overall perspective within which that belief fits. After all, there's something incongruous about holding an extreme belief content while also being generally lukewarm or noncommittal with respect to the overall perspective within which that belief resides. Similarly, there is something incongruous about being intensely committed to one's overall perspective while holding one's beliefs with a modest level of confidence. The intensification of subjects' overall commitment to their perspective is likely a crucial part of the explanation of the extremity-shift in their belief contents.

And so we find that belief polarization is a triple-edged sword. Belief polarization transforms us into more extreme versions of ourselves by prompting us to believe more extreme contents in line with our antecedent inclinations, while also intensifying our level of commitment to our perspective. And this intensification of commitment is correlated with adopting the new and more extreme belief contents with a greater degree of belief that that which we held their ancestors.

4.5 The Mechanism of Belief Polarization

We next have to investigate the mechanism driving belief polarization. Start by recalling what the experimental cases have in common: discussion among likeminded people drives discussants to shift toward extremity in the direction of their pre-discussion inclination. So, it is to be expected that when talking to likeminded others, liberals become more thoroughgoing liberals, conservatives grow more staunchly conservative, feminists shift toward a more ardent feminist position, racists intensify their racial prejudice, those advocating political protest incline toward more extreme forms political action, and so on. To repeat, the phenomenon is strikingly robust. What explains it?

There are two main theories of belief polarization's mechanism. Call the first of the two main theories the *Information View*. It begins with the observation that those engaged in discussion with likeminded others are exposed to a high concentration of affirming reasons, ideas, and "persuasive arguments."[16] It then notes that in such discussions, participants will hear novel and innovative reasons in favor of the prevailing opinion, considerations that he or she had not encountered before. This circumstance is accompanied by a corresponding scarcity within the group of articulations of countervailing or disconfirming considerations. Consequently, group members absorb the new information and revise their belief in light of it. When this revision occurs amidst the general tendency of group members to overlook the extent to which the "argument pool" from which they are drawing is skewed to favor of their position, one should expect shifts in the direction of extremity.[17] In fact, under such conditions, extremity shifts might be fully consistent with rationality, and we might in some cases have good reason to shift.

The Information View is admittedly intuitive as an account of how belief polarization works. However, it cannot be the full story. For one thing, belief polarization has been found to occur even when new and novel information is not presented in group discussion. In fact, it has been found to occur even in contexts where group interactions involve no exchange of information at all; as will be emphasized later, "mere exposure" to the fact that a group shares a general belief tendency is in some circumstances sufficient to produce the polarization.[18] Consider additionally that in likeminded groups, members who already hold an extreme view of the matter under discussion shift to an even more extreme position more drastically and more rapidly than those who begin from a more moderate stance.[19] Finally, within likeminded groups, the presence of an extremist member does not significantly amplify the polarization of the group, despite the fact that in discussion the most extreme members talk the most and speak at greater length.[20]

These findings are difficult to square with the Information View. Were it correct, one should find polarization only where information is being exchanged within the group; similarly, one should find that groups with highly vocal extremists will polarize more radically than likeminded groups of moderates, and one should also find that members of a likeminded group who are *already* extreme would tend to be less susceptible to further polarization. That said, it is not surprising that one finds enhanced polarization in instances where likeminded discussion introduces new information and novel arguments. As is well-documented, there is a general tendency among believers to *overestimate* the evidential force of novel or unexpected considerations that favor one's view.[21] But the success of this explanation of why belief polarization is especially pronounced under certain conditions does not establish that the phenomenon is fueled strictly by those processes.

The second main theory of how belief polarization works is the *Social Comparison View*. It begins by observing that members of a likeminded group tend to care about how they are perceived by the other members. In the course of discussion, they get a feel for the general tendencies within the group, and, in an effort to appear to others as neither half-hearted nor as fanatical, they each update their opinions to keep them in step with what they perceive to be the dominant tendencies. More precisely, group members revise so that their view will be seen by the others as "basically similar" to the rest of the group and yet "desirably distinctive."[22] Now, given that multiple group members are engaging simultaneously in this recalibration, and that the most fervent group members are likely to speak more in a discussion, escalating extremity naturally results. Espousing a view that reflects what one perceives to be the nonfanatical hard line within the group is a reliable way to signal one's authenticity qua group member.

One consideration in favor of the Social Comparison View is that belief polarization is enhanced in contexts where the nature of the group identity is made salient to the discussants.[23] That is, group members shift further and more rapidly toward extremity when their discussion is accompanied by an explicit acknowledgment that members do not merely agree about the matter under discussion, but also share a deeper identity. What's more, groups shift less rapidly and to a lesser extent when likeminded discussion is conducted after the recognition that the discussants are in some significant respect otherwise unalike.[24] And in mixed assemblies, once members of a subgroup are primed to see themselves as a distinct contingent within the larger whole, they are less likely to attend to statements made by those who are not members of their contingency.[25] Accordingly, the Social Comparison View has distinct advantages over the Information View. However, it too has limitations.

To be more specific, the Social Comparison View has difficulty explaining the fact that belief polarization can be activated even in the absence of anything that would count as *interaction* among the members of a group. It turns out that it is not belief recalibration in light of face-to-face *comparisons* that drive belief polarization; rather, the engine is the subject's own internal perception of the dominant tendencies within his or her identity group. In other words, although group discussions and other forms of in-person interaction among likeminded are occasions when belief polarization reliably occurs, neither information-exchange nor in-group comparison is strictly necessary for the effect. Belief polarization can occur simply when an individual is caused to feel that a group with which she identifies widely shares a view that she espouses. She need not hear any reasons in favor of the view, nor need she be in the presence of other members of the group to whom she can compare herself. The brute impression that the relevant people affirm roughly the things that she affirms suffices for an extremity shift in belief content.[26] In short, the realization that one's belief is popular among one's group suffices. Belief polarization can be initiated by means of *mere corroboration*.

To make this idea clearer, it is necessary to distinguish corroboration from *confirmation*. As the terms will be used here, confirmation involves *evidentiary* value, whereas corroboration need not contribute to one's evidence. So, when one's belief is confirmed, one obtains some new *reason* to hold it. When a belief is corroborated, by contrast, all that happens is that the belief has been given an additional affirmation. However, as the new affirmation might be based upon the very same evidence as its predecessors, it might not contribute any additional evidential support for the belief in question. Simplifying slightly, we might say that whereas confirmation adds evidence, corroboration is simply a matter of popularity, a number of voices saying "yea."[27]

Hence a third account of the mechanism driving belief polarization emerges, the *Corroboration View*. This view begins from the observation that extremity shifts can occur as a result of mere corroboration. Importantly, the corroboration can come by way of highly indirect channels. For example, being presented with data showing that liberals widely oppose genetically modified food can prompt belief polarization within liberals who already incline toward that view. Exposure to a poll showing that conservatives overwhelmingly favor a particular military action can produce an extremity shift in a conservative already disposed to favor that action.

It seems, then, that the extremity shifts of belief polarization are driven solely by the *psychological* tendency for corroboration to produce increases in one's overall commitment to one's perspective.[28] For a simplistic explanation of this that nonetheless captures fairly enough what's going on, return to the sports stadium. As was observed earlier, fandom is such a widespread phenomenon because it feels good to be part of an enthusiastic and prevailing group. In witnessing our team's victory in the presence of fellow fans, we each affirm the others' identity and commitment to the team. What's more, we each come to hold enhanced assessments of the team's excellence. As we come to regard the team as ever more talented and deserving of victory, our level of commitment to the team intensifies—we become more ardent fans.

In a similar vein, corroboration from others with whom we identify makes us feel good about what we believe.[29] When we feel good about what we believe, we experience a significant boost to our *commitment* to our overall perspective, we become a more fervent devotee to our point of view, whether it be feminist, conservative, environmentalist, egalitarian, or what have you. In turn, when that intensification happens, we are emboldened in various ways that drive us to shift to more extreme belief contents that we adopt with amplified degrees of confidence. Belief polarization can transform us into something similar to amped-up fans in the wake of a thrilling victory (or a crushing defeat).

4.6 Belief Polarization with a Humean Face

Let's pause for a moment to review. Mere corroboration suffices to induce belief polarization.[30] This indicates that although belief polarization predictably occurs in discussions and other interactions among likeminded people, these settings are not strictly necessary for the effect. The question is why corroboration is sufficient. The view on offer has it that there is a reliable psychological tendency by which corroboration of one's beliefs from a group with which one identifies intensifies one's commitment to one's perspective, and this intensification in turn leads to extremity shifts in belief contents.

An intriguing implication follows. As the relevant kind of corroboration can be indirect, extremity shifts can be induced simply by features of the social environment that make salient to individuals that some group with which they identify tends to embrace a view that they hold. These prompts need not be verbal, explicit, or literal; they can be merely implicit or subtle signals to group members that some belief is prevalent among them. Consequently, "simple attendance at certain events . . . laughter and applause at a joke . . . the wearing of political buttons or other symbolic garb or stigmata . . . may be all that is necessary to create such corroboration," and thus belief polarization.[31] Note further that as corroboration is a matter of popularity, those with the power to project the *appearance* of widespread acceptance among a particular social group of some particular view thereby have the power to induce extremity shifts among those who identify with that group. Thus belief polarization is much like the rush of fandom after all.

In light of this, return briefly to the discussion at the beginning of Chapter 3. We live in personalized social environments. Social media in particular provides us with nearly absolute power to pre-select our exposure to information and interlocutors. These platforms, and the Internet more generally, function as a kind of polarization machine.[32] And, again, our entire news and media landscape is now fused with this same technology. Thus we can see more clearly the role that "follows," "likes," and other online mechanisms (such as bots and sock puppets) play in opinion formation online: they produce the impression of identity-salient corroboration.

This provides an explanation of why online disagreement often deteriorates so rapidly. As a casual survey of almost any comments section will demonstrate, on a typical off-the-rails thread, one commenter experiences a great deal of corroboration from likeminded posters, and this results in subsequent posts escalating in extremity and confidence. At the same time, unfavorable or critical contributions are increasingly regarded as incongruous, off-point, and uninformed. Thus a flame war ensues, posters begin diagnosing each other as "trolls" and "bots," and in any case discussion is derailed. The takeaway lesson to all is to simply avoid communicating with those who do not agree with one's position. Unsurprisingly, belief polarization is rampant on social media platforms.[33] Also unsurprisingly, social media has been a boon to extremist movements, both domestically and internationally.

I take it that readers will already be familiar with the standard cautionary tales about the Internet and social media. These need not be rehashed here. The result we are now considering suggests that although the Internet might be the central site where these dysfunctions most reliably arise, there is a deeper problem that has its source in broader structures of our overall social environment. Both online and otherwise, our environments are organized around our lifestyle and identity commitments, which are now in large part constitutive of our political profiles. In making the world in our own image, we have set ourselves up for belief polarization.

As our world is also politically saturated, our social environments prompt extremity shifts in our *political* views. And so thanks to the social latitude provided by our current technology, our everyday environments are in an important respect like stadiums that we have packed with roaring fans, all rooting for our favorite political team.

This consequence will be explored in the next section. To conclude the current discussion, though, note that we have arrived at a conception of belief polarization that differs importantly from the one with which we began. To wit, belief polarization is the product not necessarily of discussion or even of interaction among likeminded people; it is rather a phenomenon that is activated when the beliefs that we hold on the basis of our salient *social identities* are corroborated by relevant others. More precisely, when we are given the impression that our beliefs are highly corroborated among the members of the social group with which we identify, we will shift into more extreme versions of ourselves. The mechanism by which this occurs is this: when something we believe is corroborated from within the relevant social group, we feel emboldened, and this intensifies our commitment to our overall perspective; this intensification in turn drives us to shift to more extreme belief contents in line with our stance. On this account, then, the mechanism driving the shift to the more extreme content is the intensification of *affect*. So, in recognition of the Scottish philosopher David Hume, who famously proclaimed that reason is the "slave of the passions," we might say that belief polarization has a *Humean* face.[34]

4.7 The Social Impact of Belief Polarization

Thus far I have been discussing belief polarization as strictly an *in-group* phenomenon, something that happens to us in virtue of our identification with a group. However, the extremity shifts of belief polarization naturally will have implications for our interactions with those who do not share our group identity. Simply put, as belief polarization changes what we think, it also changes what we think of others. To be more specific, we should expect belief polarization to be accompanied by an intensification of *negative* assessments of opposing groups, their members, and their beliefs.

Think of it this way: belief polarization initiates a broader social and political dynamic. Corroboration from the relevant identity group increases our overall level of commitment to our perspective and prompts us to adopt more extreme beliefs in line with our antecedent identity commitments. From the standpoint of that intensified outlook, opposing views and countervailing considerations are bound to appear distorted, feeble, ill-founded, and extraneous. To employ an image that hopefully is not too farfetched, the belief polarization phenomenon operates almost like the side-view mirror on an automobile; it consolidates our firstpersonal perspective and makes everything else appear distant and disfigured. As belief polarization takes effect, we come not only to believe firmly things that are further out of step with our evidence, we thereby also lose sensitivity to the force of the reasons that drive the views of our opponents and critics.

Accordingly, once we are sufficiently belief-polarized, those who espouse views that differ from ours will strike us as more and more alien, benighted, incoherent, and perhaps even unintelligible. Thus the intellectual distance separating us from others will seem to expand momentously, and indeed, those who hold views that run directly contrary to our own will strike us as irrational extremists, people devoted to views that make little sense and enjoy no support.[35] What's more, as the opposition grows more unintelligible to us, their views will also come to look to us as increasingly simplistic and monolithic. Consequently, we will be prone to conclude that their ideas, arguments, and criticisms are wholly without merit and thus not worth engaging, and we might even actively avoid contact with them. We will grow more inclined to see those who hold views that differ from ours to be in need of *diagnosis* and *treatment* rather than reasons and arguments. Of course, all of this only more firmly ensconces us within our own likeminded group, which in turn further entrenches our group identity and enhances belief polarization, driving us to further extremity.

I take it that this dynamic is familiar. We have all *seen* it befall others. Recall some of the data discussed in Chapter 3, where it was found not only that social spaces are increasingly sorted according to partisan political identities, but also that this segmentation has been accompanied by an exaggerated sense of the depth of our partisan division as well as intensified antipathy across partisan divides.[36] It was also noted that this antipathy has risen to such a pitch that partisan citizens now report that the opposing party causes them anger and anxiety. Moreover, citizens more commonly regard the ideas of their political opponents as not simply misguided, but positive *threats* to the country.[37] Recalling the discussion from earlier in this chapter, we can say that sorting has been accompanied by increased affective political polarization.

Consider next the more general result from Chapter 3 that our social spaces are not only sorted, but also politically saturated. This means that our workaday experiences are inundated with appeals to our political identities—sometimes overt and explicit, other times barely liminal. In any case, casual social experience increasingly reinforces our political identities, and simultaneously punctuates our distance from those who inhabit social identities that differ from our own. And as we have seen, these appeals often operate by first making salient some political identity and then indicating an attitude or behavior that one is expected to have on the basis of embracing that identity. Given the Corroboration View, this suffices to induce belief polarization.

So our politically saturated social environments are also breeding grounds for extremity shifts in our political views. As those shifts involve amplifications of our overall confidence in our political perspectives, they also produce intensifications of our political identities. And, as our political identities are now fused with our social identities in the broadest sense, our social spaces breed belief polarization with respect to our commitments of all kinds.

We consequently are more prone to see political significance in ordinary social behavior that is arguably nonpolitical; we explain more of what others do by appealing to their political allegiances. One result of this is that we tend to exhibit distrust in the general capacities of those who do not share our politics, even when it comes to those who are experts in tasks that do not involve political judgment.[38] But more importantly, as we become more extreme versions of ourselves with respect to our political views, we also produce conditions that support political polarization of the three kinds catalogued earlier in this chapter. To wit, as we become more extreme versions of ourselves as political believers, we also increase uniformity within our political group, intensify our distrust of those who are different, and create progressively deeper affective rifts across partisan divides.

Again, all of this occurs within a self-reinforcing and downward-spiraling dynamic. Politically saturated social environments induce belief polarization, which in turn produces political polarization in all of its forms. This reinforces the saturation, resulting in further belief and political polarization. We are caught in a self-fulfilling cycle of dysfunction. And we actually become more like what our most vehement political opponents think of us, and they grow more closely to fit our distorted images of them. And on it goes.

4.8 The Diagnostic Argument Completed

That these results pose a significant threat to democracy perhaps goes without saying. Still, we have arrived at this diagnosis by way of an arduous path. It makes sense, then, to conclude Part II by reviewing our findings.

Our social environments are politically saturated. This means that our spaces are socially sorted, and, as politics has become tightly fused with our broader social identities, our everyday activities are increasingly taken to be enactments of our political commitments. The result is that we engage more and more in acts that are imbued with political significance, but nearly always under conditions that are socially homogeneous. Hence our activities qua citizens are rarely engaged with those whose political commitments differ from our own.

This is already a challenging circumstance for democracy. Part of what drives a democracy toward political saturation is the idea that democracy is fundamentally a society of publicly engaged citizens who must govern themselves as equals, despite their ongoing disagreements about the precise shape the political world should take. The distinctively democratic idea is that, given the persistence of this kind of disagreement among citizens, politics must be guided by processes that afford to each an equal role in deciding public policy. As was argued in Chapter 2, the political equality that democracy calls for involves more than an equal vote; in a democracy, citizens must have an equal *say*, and this requires that they have the opportunity to be *heard* as equals by their fellow citizens and also by their government. In this way, citizens can come to understand each other's political opinions and the rationales that underwrite them. When mutual understanding of this kind is attained, citizens can then fruitfully disagree, contest each other's views, and hold one another accountable, along with their representatives and their government. Only under such conditions can political governance plausibly be regarded as something beyond the brute imposition of coercive power. Put otherwise, when political decision is guided by the public engagement of the citizens, the exercise of political power is rendered consistent with their equality. Even though coercive power nonetheless will be exercised on behalf of a political decision that some citizens do not support (and might even staunchly oppose), no one is reduced to the status of a subordinate.

That is the democratic ideal, anyway. Political saturation frustrates this core aspiration. Under such conditions, there is an abundance of political communication, but very little occasion to listen to or be heard by those who politically are unlike ourselves. We preach incessantly, but nearly always only to our own choir. Thus we gain a heightened—indeed, exaggerated—sense of our political divides, and we also lose sight of the rationales driving our opposition's views (they lose sight of ours, too). Politics consequently becomes all the more argumentative while proper argument is rendered nearly impossible. As a result, collective political decisions are prone to be experienced as merely *imposed* on some by others. Democracy degenerates into a cold war among citizens.

Surely a *cold* war among democratic citizens is preferable to a *hot* one. In the previous chapter, we considered briefly an alternative account that might hold that although it would be *better* for citizens to be less clustered into politically homogeneous spaces and more able to interact across partisan divisions, there's nothing particularly *threatening* to democracy in the existing state of affairs. Perhaps an orderly and stable cold war among citizens is the best that democracy can achieve?

We are now positioned to respond fully to this line of argument. The envisioned argument would be more compelling, perhaps, were it not the case that there is reason to think that a cold war among democratic citizens is unstable. The belief polarization results that have been presented in this chapter indicate that our politically saturated social spaces set in motion a dynamic by which, through public political engagement that indeed may be sincere and well-intentioned, we nevertheless progressively shift into more extreme versions of ourselves. This in turn exacerbates our political divisions in ways that further intensify political extremity. To be more precise, the belief polarization phenomenon does not merely transform us into more extreme versions of ourselves; it also turns us into people who are less capable of dealing reasonably with people who are unlike us. This dismantles our democratic capacities.

To see this, recall once again that the democratic ideal of self-government among equals can be pursued only when citizens can engage in collective reasoning about their shared political order. This means that citizens must be able to access each other's reasons and engage in processes of exchange that include criticizing, arguing, questioning, and objecting to one another's views as well as to the views of their public officials and the acts of their government. Belief polarization is a phenomenon by which extremity shifts in belief content and overall commitment are driven not by reasons, but by mere corroboration of beliefs that one holds on the basis of one's social identity. Thus, those subject to belief polarization wind up with views that they cannot adequately support with reasons; moreover, they are also less able to competently engage with the reasons of others. In short, belief polarization produces extremity shifts in our belief contents and in our overall commitment to our viewpoints, but it does not provide us with correspondingly better arguments, reasons, or evidence. To the contrary, the phenomenon leaves us generally in a cognitively *worse* position than we are likely to have been in prior to the effect. Once belief-polarized, we believe more confidently things that we are less able to support with reasons. Crucially, we are also less inclined to consider disconfirming ideas, more inclined merely to dismiss those who offer them, more prone to see those who do not share our views as incompetent extremists, and also more inclined to dig our heels in when presented with reason to reassess our views.

This is the fundamental problem posed by polarization. Belief polarization directly attacks our capacities to properly enact democratic citizenship, dissolving our abilities to treat our fellow citizens as our political equals. Moreover, belief polarization is part of a larger dynamic by which partisan divisions expand and extremity intensifies, all within a structure of self-perpetuating social dysfunction. It is difficult to see how this path produces anything other than mounting political distrust, cynicism, and incivility. And these are no doubt accompanied by an amplified willingness to use power to impose one's political will on the rest.

The philosopher Alasdair MacIntyre once characterized democracy as "civil war carried on by other means."[39] This is, perhaps, an apt depiction of the real world of democracy under normal social conditions. That real-world democracy falls short of the ideal of self-government among equals is to be expected. The analysis presented here, though, shows that democracy is falling short in a different sense: democracy is moving *further* from the ideal and toward its own collapse. That is, our current circumstances provide the conditions by which "civil war carried on by other means" threatens to degenerate into a civil war carried on by the typical means.

Return finally to the central theme of overdoing democracy and the corresponding need to put politics in its place. To be sure, democratic political movements can coalesce only when citizens gather with likeminded others to form coalitions and action groups; indeed, the successful social justice movements of our day have depended upon the kind of coordination and galvanization that can occur only when likeminded people can work together outside of the view and involvement of others. The foregoing argument has neither denied nor denounced that feature of democratic political action. The problem does not lie with political coalitions and sustained efforts to mobilize them. The trouble rather is that our social spaces *as such* are politically saturated, and therefore they are breeding grounds for belief polarization and its corresponding degenerative ramifications, as reflected in the polarization dynamic. Our everyday activities serve as prompts for the intensification and radicalization of our political identities, which in turn exacerbate our political divisions.

Nonetheless we remain democratic citizens and must take responsibility for the political world we share. Given the challenges that our democracy presently confronts (including the standing injustices that demand political redress), wholesale withdrawal from politics is not morally permissible. Yet our political engagements, however sincere and well-intentioned, expose us to forces that will likely degrade our democratic capacities and accelerate democracy's deterioration. We find ourselves mired in political quicksand.

The instinctual reflex among conscientious citizens to meet political dysfunctions with more concentrated political action must be tempered. In the absence of additional interventions, intensified political activity is likely to exacerbate the trouble. The problem we face is not that we are neglecting democratic politics, nor is it that we are enacting democratic politics in the wrong way. The problem rather is that politics has become *all that we do together*. Thus further entrenchment into politics only feeds the polarization dynamic. We confront a political problem that is native to democracy and yet does not admit of a political solution.

Hence an exasperating conundrum. If politics isn't the solution to this problem with democracy, what else is there? How could there be a nonpolitical solution to a political problem? Dwelling for a moment on what's confounding in this may prove helpful in envisioning a way forward.

I observed in Chapter 1 that we are intuitively attracted to an idea that is often associated with two of the greatest democratic thinkers of the twentieth century, Jane Addams and John Dewey. They held that the cure for democracy's ills is always more—meaning fuller—democracy. In fact, Dewey affirmed something stronger than this. He asserted the principle that "democratic ends require democratic methods for their realization"; this entails that there could be no remedy for a problem with democracy that is not itself an exercise of democratic politics.[40] I have argued here that democracy suffers from an ailment for which democracy cannot be a remedy.

Dewey's principle overlooks the possibility that there are social means for enriching democracy that are *not democratic*, because they are not political at all. Put differently, Dewey did not recognize that democracy could be stunted *internally*, that is, from our exaggerated pursuit of the democratic ideal. Recall the discussion in Chapter 1 of Alice, the physical fitness enthusiast. Alice winds up undermining her goal not because she pursues fitness to an insufficient extent; rather, she fails because she pursues physical fitness to the exclusion of all other goods. In this way, she distorts her pursuit by achieving it in a way that undermines its *point*.

In adopting the Addams/Dewey line, we tend to overlook the fact that some good things derive their value in part from other goods that are obtained and enriched when the first good is properly secured. Accordingly, there are ways of failing at certain good pursuits that owe to the *single-mindedness* of our effort. My contention is that democracy is a social good of this kind.

We might better capture this by saying that democracy is subject to a kind of autoimmune disorder. Democracy can be enacted in a way that crowds out and eventually suffocates other social goods whose realization is both necessary for democracy's flourishing and part of the point of democratic politics. In this chapter and its predecessor, I argued that certain social and technological forces have resulted in a circumstance where our sincere and vigilant democratic efforts backfire. Our earnest democratic engagements invigorate the polarization dynamic, which in turn disassembles our democratic capacities.

Our tendency to overlook the possibility of a political "autoimmune" dysfunction is what makes the very idea of a political problem for which democracy cannot be a solution confounding. And, to be frank, I'm not certain that there is a solution to the problem of overdoing democracy. But the argument thus far has shown that if there is a solution, it must reside outside of politics. There are some democratic ends that require *nondemocratic* (because nonpolitical) means for their realization.

According to the proposal to be developed in the remainder of this book, the cure for this particular ailment facing our democracy is to do something other than democracy. The way forward is to devise social venues of nonpolitical cooperative endeavor, sites where we can interact in ways that do not invoke our partisan profiles, spaces where politics is not simply set aside, but instead has no place. By engaging in collaborative activities of this kind, we might be able to escape the polarization dynamic. I concede that the very idea of a nonpolitical social cooperative endeavor strikes us as alien, perhaps even incoherent. But I repeat that the peculiarity of this idea is itself a manifestation of our tendency to overdo democracy, to regard politics as necessarily all-consuming. In any case, I have made the case that we must put politics in its place. It is the task of subsequent chapters to make sense of how we might go about doing so.

PART III
PRESCRIPTION

5

Civic Friendship

Here is where things stand. The preceding two chapters made the case for thinking that in the United States and other modern democratic societies, democracy is being overdone, and this is detrimental to democracy. The upshot is that given the political saturation of our social environments and our persistent vulnerability to belief polarization, even our most conscientious political engagements aimed at enriching and improving democracy are likely to contribute further to degenerative political dysfunctions. It goes without saying that our most common modes of political engagement are not especially conscientious and are more often aimed at furthering narrowly partisan objectives than enriching democracy as such. Consequently, the portrait of contemporary democracy that has emerged is unrelentingly bleak. With that diagnosis in place, it is now time to develop a prescription.

The shape of my proposal already has been indicated. Politics must be put in its place, and we can do this by participating together in cooperative social endeavors that are fundamentally nonpolitical in nature. Thus far my formulations of this proposal have served principally to disambiguate it from certain other ideas for which it might be mistaken. Hence what has been presented in the foregoing pages has been partial and vague. It is time to provide the requisite details.

A familiar difficulty emerges instantly. According to the diagnostic argument, our political allegiances and identities are built into the very structure of our social environments. Does it not follow from this that *anything* we might do together must be inescapably political in precisely the sense that is to be avoided? Hasn't the argument painted us into a corner, leaving no room in which to build a prescription? I see this as an especially formidable challenge. But one sure way to fail to meet it would be to begin by prescribing nonpolitical activities for citizens to begin participating in together. Any item on a list of nonpolitical activities justifiably will provoke the objection that it is merely an expression of some political leaning or profile; thus the original problem of overdoing democracy simply reemerges.

I learned this during a public presentation I gave shortly after I first started working on these themes. In a Q&A period, I was asked by a sympathetic audience member to recommend a collective activity that could help put politics in its place. My response was that citizens might volunteer together to clean litter from a public park. A less sympathetic audience member retorted that this activity is "liberal." In reply, I stated that it was not clear how removing litter from a public park could be plausibly regarded as a political endeavor, let alone one that is distinctively liberal. After all, isn't the undesirability of litter something about which everyone agrees, regardless of political affiliation—and, indeed, independent of political affiliation? I posed that question and moved on to the next. It later occurred to me that I hadn't taken the challenge seriously enough. I had assumed that the audience member was alleging that cleaning litter is liberal, but perhaps the claim rather was that *volunteering* is a strictly liberal enterprise? Or maybe the thought was that volunteering to clean a park with one's *neighbors* (rather than, say, with fellow congregants from one's church) is distinctively liberal? Another possibility is that the interlocutor was contending that prioritizing the endeavor of cleaning a park over other, arguably more pressing, social needs is liberal. I'll never know. In any case, in my attempt to propose a concrete plan for putting politics in its place, I merely reinstated the problem of overdoing democracy. I failed to see a political valence in volunteering to clean a park, whereas a fellow citizen saw a very clear political leaning in the proposal.

The crucial lesson is that the problem of overdoing democracy cannot be solved with an itinerary of nonpolitical activities for citizens to engage in. Alas, the fix to the problem is not so easy. Putting politics in its place requires us to change our view of politics itself. Accordingly, concrete proposals for nonpolitical collective activities must not be offered prematurely. In order to address the problem of overdoing democracy adequately, we must take an indirect route. To better understand why this is so, let's begin by considering an attempt to address the problem directly.

5.1 The Better Democracy Response

It might seem that the problem of overdoing democracy admits of an obvious fix. If, as I have insisted, the problem of overdoing democracy does not lie in the frequency and intensity of our political activity, but rather in the fact that, wittingly or otherwise, we enact our politics perpetually and nearly always within homogeneous spaces, then it might seem obvious that a proper response is to create *heterogeneous* spaces within which political activity can be engaged. According to this kind of view, the problem of overdoing democracy is in actuality the problem of overdoing an inadequately democratic mode of politics. Thus the solution is to make our politics more authentically democratic.

This can be regarded as a reformulation of the Addams/Dewey injunction to respond to democratic ailments always with more democracy. The reformulation consists in taking *more* to mean not only fuller, but also better. Following this line, one might think that once better conditions for political engagement are instituted, improvements to democratic practice will follow organically from ordinary political interactions. Call this intuitive and reassuring idea the *Better Democracy* response.

Something like this proposal animates the research programs associated with deliberative democracy. The deliberativists contend that when discourse is conducted within a properly democratic context, the polarization dynamic is broken and the corresponding dysfunctions are annulled—discussants do not shift to extremes, common ground materializes, mutual respect is regained, principled agreements are reached, and democracy revitalizes.[1] As they see it, the task is to construct properly democratic venues for political discourse and incentivize citizens to interact within them.

Of course, there are competing theories of what makes a venue for engagement properly democratic; thus there are also disputes about how to design such a venue. As was noted in Chapter 2, some deliberative views call for far-reaching departures from ordinary modes of democratic politics, urging the creation of new large-scale institutions and fundamental changes to the political order. One notorious proposal along these lines recommends that we instate a new national holiday dedicated to nationwide deliberation events; another proposes the establishment—by means of a change to the US Constitution—of a fourth, "deliberative" branch of government.[2] Other theorists of this stripe look to more modest interventions, such as the introduction into common democratic practice of small-scale deliberative exercises, variously construed as mini-publics, citizen juries, and citizen assemblies.[3] Pruning further still, some have called centrally for policy initiatives, such as laws requiring radically partisan web pages to carry links to opponents' sites.[4] The deliberativists' proposals for better democracy are too numerous to catalogue here. What they have in common is the claim that if we can construct proper conditions for people to enact democracy, the dysfunctions I have identified either will completely subside or else become more tractable and less politically debilitating.

The Better Democracy response of the deliberative democrats is worth considering carefully because, as some readers will have observed, the argument throughout this book has employed the conception of democratic political legitimacy that lies at the heart of most versions of deliberative democracy. To repeat, according to that conception, political power is legitimately exercised only when it is consistent with a due acknowledgment of the freedom and equality of all citizens; and the requisite kind of acknowledgment is manifest only when political decision is responsive to processes by which citizens' voices—their reasons, arguments, ideas, objections, and criticisms—are given a hearing and engaged with, both by fellow citizens and by government officials. The dysfunctions I have focused on are plausibly seen as deriving from breakdowns in processes of public political discourse. The proposed solution, then, is to enact democracy under conditions specially designed to foster proper exchanges among citizens within heterogeneous deliberative groups.

Several decades of experimental work on political deliberation within specially designed democratic spaces has produced a great deal of data, much of which is highly encouraging. According to some results, participating in a deliberation experiment has long-term positive consequences for one's political behavior and civic engagement. Other data suggest that participation in a curated discussion among citizens who are ideologically diverse tends to moderate polarization, and shift discussants away from extremity. Accordingly, an industry has emerged of civic engagement experts and public deliberation facilitators, all offering programs for enhancing democracy within groups of all sizes.

All of this is promising, and nothing in the prescription I will be advancing strictly opposes interventions of these kinds. In fact, my view is that the development of fora where democratic deliberation can be better conducted among citizens and officials is to be encouraged. Why would anyone oppose interventions aimed at improving democracy? However, recall that the Better Democracy proposal holds that improving the environments where democratic activities occur is *sufficient* for addressing the problem of overdoing democracy and its resultant dysfunctions. That is where the Better Democracy proposals fail. Better Democracy initiatives, in the form of enhanced deliberation venues, do not suffice as a solution to the problem of overdoing democracy, and in the absence of measures of another kind they may even exacerbate it.

The first thing to note about the public deliberation experiments is that the data they have produced are not univocal. Whereas it is true that in some cases, curated public deliberation indeed seems to have resulted in important democratic and civic enhancements among participants, there are other experiments in which politically heterogeneous discussion seems instead to have only fortified existing tendencies. In fact, in some settings, heterogeneous discussion has been found to exacerbate polarization, further entrench the unflattering stereotypes that participants harbor of their political opposition, and intensify perceived partisan differences.[5]

Along similar lines, some data indicate that, following participation in deliberation experiments, citizens report an increased likeliness to participate in political processes that they otherwise would have skipped. Yet there are also findings suggesting that political deliberation suppresses political participation, and vice versa. That is, there is reason to think that citizens who follow the deliberative democrats' directive to engage regularly in political dialogue with politically heterogeneous others are rendered by such encounters less likely to participate in political activities, including voting. And the same results indicate the converse, namely that political interaction among likeminded others *encourages* political activity. According to these results, we can promote democratically responsible public deliberation *or* enthusiastic political participation, but not both.[6]

These matters need not be canvassed further. It is not surprising that experimental data regarding socially complex phenomena are multivalent. And one should expect data of that kind to provoke ongoing academic debates over their proper interpretation. The upshot at present is that in the midst of these debates over varied data, one should decline to adopt a proposed solution to the problem of overdoing democracy that relies so heavily on one particular interpretation of those data. This is perhaps especially evident in light of the findings that suggest that the impact of participation in democratic deliberation depends largely on the antecedent attitudes and dispositions of the deliberators. Those who bring to the deliberation an appreciation for civil political disagreement and a desire to cooperate across political divides will usually benefit from participation, whereas those who enter the discussion with less favorable views of the enterprise will likely have their tendencies and biases confirmed, and possibly amplified.[7] Recall that the problem of overdoing democracy is in part the problem of restoring in citizens the disposition concerning political disagreement and cooperation that would make deliberation beneficial. We have reason to think that when it comes to experimental deliberative settings, what one puts in determines what one gets out.

The experimental results we have been considering occasion an additional critical response. Many of the deliberative democracy experiments seek explicitly to address a particular kind of objection that is quite different from the concern raised by the problem of overdoing democracy. To be more specific, much of the empirical work on public deliberation is aimed at responding to various kinds of *skepticism* about deliberative democracy. This skepticism sometimes is expressed as doubt that citizens care to participate in public deliberation; other times, it is articulated as the suspicion that ordinary citizens are cognitively incapable of reaping any benefits from deliberation. Both versions are often accompanied by the related claim that there is no benefit to democratic politics to be gained by public deliberation.

Deliberation experiments are often designed to show that citizens have both the interest in political deliberation and the competence to make deliberation politically worthwhile.[8] Hence the significance of these experiments is not diluted by the fact that the artificial conditions under which they enact deliberation are markedly distant from those under which real-world political talk occurs.

Deliberative democrats can (and often do) acknowledge with the skeptics that political talk in the real world is democratically debilitating. They aspire to show by means of their experiments not that real-world political talk is properly deliberative, but that the faults with real-world political discourse are not insurmountable, that ordinary citizens, once situated within a properly democratic setting, are up to the task of deliberative politics.

The challenge posed by overdoing democracy is different from the challenge presented by the deliberative democracy skeptics. Hence the empirical work that is aimed at counteracting that skepticism does not address the problem being raised here. That there are conditions under which political deliberation amongst ordinary citizens reliably produces significant democratic benefits is an encouraging result. But the concern at present has to do with citizens interacting almost exclusively within politically saturated social spaces. In the real world of political engagement, spaces are not heterogeneous and communication is not structured according to the tenets of well-developed theories of democratic discourse. Moreover, as was argued in Chapter 3, potent forms of political communication do not manifest as explicit reasons, arguments, or even statements uttered; rather, political communication occurs commonly by way of various kinds of *signals* of group identity. And the Corroboration View of belief polarization defended in Chapter 4 entails that environmental features suffice to induce extremity shifts. To repeat, all that is needed to induce belief polarization is a prompt that makes salient to us that a belief that we hold is prevalent among those who share our social identity. Isolated and sporadic episodes in which politically diverse citizens are guided by facilitators to engage in properly democratic deliberation can hardly be expected to offset the impact of widespread political saturation on our beliefs and attitudes.

Now a deeper issue comes into view. Discussions of the deliberation experiments conducted in support of the Better Democracy proposal often overlook a crucial distinction between *preventing* belief polarization and *reversing* it. In fact, the intuitive force of the Better Democracy idea frequently derives from a conflation of these two.[9] To explain, it is obvious that one way to solve the problems for democracy that belief polarization poses is to eliminate the conditions under which belief polarization arises. But that truism says nothing about the problem of overdoing democracy, which is the problem of conducting democracy after belief polarization has risen to dangerous levels. To use a medical analogy, the prevention of a disease is distinct from its cure. It may be true that the Better Democracy initiatives of the deliberative democrats are adequate to *prevent* democracy's ills. What is required, though, is a treatment for the malady of overdoing democracy.

To put this point in a different way, the deliberative experiments suggest that proper deliberation—professionally managed discussion that is structured according to norms of inclusion and civility, within a heterogeneous group—can prevent belief polarization. However, this welcome result seems prevalent among only those discussants who have not already formulated a strong and identity-infused opinion about some political issue; with such subjects, facilitated discussion of that issue with a heterogeneous group can indeed prevent the formation of extreme attitudes, and may even help to shift individuals' existing beliefs in the direction of moderation. But this does not entail that facilitated discussion within a heterogeneous group is the "solution" to belief polarization.[10] What is required rather is a way to *depolarize* those who have already been subjected to belief polarization. And just as the Corroboration View of belief polarization predicts, when it comes to subjects who enter the conversation with firm opinions that they associate with their salient group identity, discussion within heterogeneous groups tends to *intensify* their extremity.[11] Under existing conditions, then, exhorting citizens to practice better democracy of the kind envisioned by the deliberative democrats will not contribute to depolarization and might well further fuel the polarization dynamic. So, although experiments designed to involve citizens in contexts that better approximate ideal democratic deliberation are welcome, they are not sufficient. A solution to the problem of overdoing democracy must be sought elsewhere.

5.2 The Circumstances of Politics

Once again, we must go back to square one. It has been claimed repeatedly that democracy is the ideal of self-government among equals. Up to this point, discussion of this ideal has emphasized that if political decision-making is to be consistent with the equality of all citizens, it must be responsive to their voices—their concerns, criticisms, reasons, and arguments—and not simply their votes. Although the preceding chapters have projected a bleak image of real-world democracy, that bleakness owes largely to the contrasting majesty of the democratic ideal. Who could deny that there is something dignifying in the ideal of self-government among equals? It is easy to wax rhapsodic in extolling the democratic vision of life and society. Nevertheless, if we are to respond to the problem of overdoing democracy we must not allow ourselves to become captivated by the ideal.

We do not often dwell on it, but democracy is hard to love. After all, democracy is in part the curious thesis that there are political conditions under which forcing a person to live according to rules that she rejects is nevertheless consistent with a due recognition of her status as an equal. Consider further that democracy is additionally the proposal that she may be rightfully forced to live according to rules that are supported only by others who are justifiably regarded as ignorant, misinformed, deluded, corrupt, irrational, or worse. Further, it is the proposal that she may be rightfully forced to live according to rules that are favored by the majority when those rules are favored because of the majority's ignorance and irrationality. And under democracy, a citizen may be rightfully forced to live according to the rules favored by a majority of her fellow citizens even though she is able to demonstrate that they are ignorant and irrational, and despite the fact that she can debunk the rationales they offer in support of the rules that they favor. Further still, democracy involves the contention that such a citizen may be rightfully forced to live according to rules favored by a demonstrably irrational and ignorant majority even if she is able to show that were the majority slightly less irrational and ignorant, they would fervently support wholly different rules.

Yet another bleak depiction! But it is crucial to note that the foregoing does not describe some dysfunctional existing democracy. I've been describing democracy in the ideal, democracy *at its best*. To repeat: Even in the ideal, democracy is the proposal that those who find themselves on the losing end of a democratic decision must nonetheless abide by it, even though they might be able to impugn the rationales by which the prevailing option gained favor among its advocates. Under perfect democratic conditions, someone who finds herself in the democratic minority is bound by the majority judgment, even though it might be significantly flawed in demonstrable ways.

Everybody knows that the real-world democracy is far from the ideal. In real-world democracies, citizens are indeed forced to live according to rules that are favored by ignorant, misinformed, and irrational citizens; and many of the rules we live by are defensible only by way of the flawed rationales embraced by our ignorant fellows. Moreover, concerted and sincere attempts to rationally sway the majority in the direction of better policies often fail; that is, the irrationality and ignorance of the majority is stunningly resilient. So, in real-world democracy, well-informed citizens are politically at the mercy of their irrational and ignorant fellow citizens. Knowing this, politicians and officials strategically cater to majority irrationality, and, once in power, they govern for the sake of gaining reelection.

Back in Chapter 2, there was occasion to consider briefly the position of those who find themselves on the losing side of a democratic vote. In order to build toward a prescription for dealing with the problem of overdoing democracy, we must turn more fully to issues that are raised by the fact that whenever democracy decides, somebody *loses*.

Democracy is many things—a moral ideal, a kind of society, a way of life, an instrument for social justice, a mechanism for making collective decisions, and so on. But democracy always is also a mode of politics. And politics is always in part a matter of exercising coercive power, power designed to induce people to do things that they might not otherwise do, might not want to do, and might think that they should not have to do. Indeed, politics sometimes involves the exercise of power to force people to do things that they think it is wrong for them to do. Accordingly, even under highly favorable conditions, politics is messy, conflicted business.

Democracy is the thesis that it is nonetheless possible to conduct politics in a way that respects the fundamental equality of those over whom coercive power is exercised. One might think that the imposition of such power is consistent with the citizens' equality only when there is *unanimity* among them regarding how the power should be deployed. Democracy involves the emphatic denial of this thought. Democracy involves the claim that under certain conditions, a citizen's equality is adequately respected even whilst coercive political power is employed to force her to do what she does not want to do. We can capture this fundamental premise underlying democratic politics like this: Legitimate government is possible among equal citizens who disagree over how political power should be wielded. Or, put differently, unanimity among equal citizens regarding how political power should be exercised is not necessary in order for exercises of that power to be legitimate.

As usual, there are important questions afoot that will be set aside. The point is that democracy is premised on the idea that politics can be conducted legitimately even amidst ongoing political disagreements among its citizens. In fact, democracy embraces the further claim that persistent political disagreement among citizens is to be expected under conditions of equality and freedom. And some theorists go so far as to say that such disagreement is itself a *manifestation* of the freedom and equality of democratic citizens. As was discussed in Chapter 2, classical views of democracy aspire to demonstrate how a stable political system can manage and contain disagreements of that kind; public engagement views, by contrast, model democracy in ways that construe ongoing political disagreements as positive contributions to the legitimacy of the democratic order. In any case, democracy is a proposal for legitimate politics—which always involves the exercise of coercive force—under perpetual, unyielding political dissensus among equal citizens.

It might be said, then, that according to any democratic view ineradicable political dissensus among equals is one of the brute facts of politics. Borrowing a term from discussions of distributive justice, we can say that such dissensus is one of the *circumstances of politics*. This is to say that ongoing political disagreement is at once a feature of political life that any conception of politics must account for and part of the reason why we need a political order at all. Put simply, were it not for the fact of persistent disagreement, we would have no need to theorize politics because there would be no need for a political order in the first place. Politics is a response to persistent disagreement.

It should be emphasized that democracy presupposes that citizens will disagree not only about the direction that exercises of political power should take, but also about the point and objective of such exercises. That is, it is expected that citizens will disagree about the *ends* of politics and not simply the means. Hence citizens will disagree not only about, say, how justice is best achieved, but also about what justice is. To be sure, disagreements of these fundamental kinds are subject to certain constraints; for example, holding that justice requires the systematic oppression of some citizens by others is inconsistent with the equality upon which democracy is premised. Citizens who embrace antidemocratic conceptions of justice raise fascinating problems for political legitimacy, but discussion of these would take us too far afield. Nonetheless, it is expected that within a democratic citizenry, one will find a broad range of opposing views concerning what the central political values of freedom, justice, autonomy, and the like amount to. In short, among the circumstances of politics is dissensus that is normatively *deep*.

Once it is recognized that political dissensus of a certain normative depth is among the circumstances of politics, we find that political loss is an additional ineliminable feature of the political order; such loss is also among the circumstances of politics. It is important to grasp the full impact of this point. Democratic politics is not simply a competition among different and opposed preferences or desires regarding the exercise of political power. To be sure, democracy does involve competing preferences and desires; however, democracy also involves *conflicts of value*. Citizens commonly understand their political views as deriving from their deeper convictions about right and wrong, fairness and unfairness, justice and injustice, and so on. This means that in certain political decision contexts, something more than a preference is at stake. More precisely, citizens advocate, petition, organize, argue, campaign, and vote for the sake of aligning the political world with their values. Accordingly, it is not only that citizens seek to get the political results they favor; they favor the particular results they do because they see them as required by their deeper moral commitments.

This helps explain why democratic politics is so often acrimonious and volatile. In a democracy, political decisions must be reached, but, as dissensus is a brute fact, whenever a decision is made, some citizens lose while others win. And this winning and losing is often not simply a matter of getting or failing to get one's way. A citizen who finds herself on the losing side of a democratic vote might regard the prevailing option as not simply suboptimal, but as objectionable. The loss will then be experienced not merely as a disappointment or frustration, but also as an *affront*. And yet, provided that the decision was arrived at in the right way and satisfies certain other substantive requirements (it must not violate civil rights, for example), she is required to accede to the result; in most contexts, this means that she must obey rules and directives that she believes are normatively incorrect.

That properly democratic political outcomes are binding on citizens does not mean that those who oppose a particular outcome must silently bear the imposition. Democracy permits channels by which even after a decision has been made by way of proper processes, citizens may continue to argue, advocate, instigate, and campaign against it. And in certain circumstances, democracy also recognizes the permissibility of forms of active resistance, including protest, refusal, and civil disobedience. As was noted in Chapter 2, democracy's claim to reconcile the exercise of political power with the equality of those over whom it is exercised depends crucially on the avenues it affords to citizens for ongoing disputation, critique, and advocacy. Thus even when democracy produces a result that affronts a citizen's values, she is entitled to continue pressing for redress, revision, and reversal; in this way, her coercion is consistent with her status as an equal.

This is of course a highly simplified account of democratic legitimacy. But it suffices to bring into view a crucial point. The dual circumstances of politics that have been identified—dissensus and loss—entail that the success of democracy depends on citizens' capacity to sustain their investment in democratic processes even in the wake of what they might regard as momentous normative lapses and errors. Put otherwise, democracy needs citizens who can remain faithful to democratic politics even when democracy produces results that they regard as morally flawed, or even unconscionable.

To grasp this, simply note that the avenues of redress and recourse that democracy offers to citizens who are aggrieved all presuppose that the democratic society at large will remain receptive to their objections, protests, criticisms, and reasons. In order for citizens to perceive the point of engaging in democratic forms of criticism and redress, they must retain a certain stance toward their fellow citizens. More specifically, even in the wake of what they consider a seriously flawed democratic outcome, citizens must be able to regard their compatriots as good-faith democratic actors who can be moved by reasons, objections, and proposals for revision; they must be able to *trust* that their compatriots will continue to act as democratic citizens. When citizens are incapable of trusting each other in this way, there is little (if any) reason to regard a given democratic outcome as anything but the brute exercise of power by some over others; thus there is little (if any) reason to pursue democratic methods for redress of political grievances.

So democracy is not only hard to love; it is also plain hard. It is not easy to sustain one's investment in democratic politics in the wake of a political outcome that one considers normatively deplorable. Perhaps it is even more difficult to sustain one's trust in one's fellow citizens when one regards as deeply normatively flawed a political outcome that is widely favored among them. The result is that democracy needs citizens to be possessed of certain capacities that enable them to manage the inevitable political losses that come with a democratic political order, skills that enable them to sustain their investment in democracy even when democracy produces political results that affront their values.

5.3 Civic Friends and Civic Enmity

The next item of business is to identify the requisite democratic capacities. For reasons that will become clear later in this section, it will suffice to begin with a rough sketch. It has already been noted that in order to sustain our investment in democracy in the wake of political loss, we must be able to trust our fellow citizens to be responsive to our reasons, willing to consider objections, capable of envisioning alternatives, prepared to revise their views in light of criticisms, and so on. We must be able to trust that, after a democratic decision is reached, those who are pleased by the result will regard those who have sustained a political loss as nevertheless fully citizens who are entitled to continue pressing for reform and revision. The requirement that democratic citizens have not only a voice but also a hearing does not expire after the votes are counted. So as democratic citizens we must have the capacities to listen to challenges to our own commitments, to address the criticisms posed by our fellow citizens, to provide reasons in favor of our views, and to revise our ideas when necessary. These are centrally *cognitive* abilities, having to do with the ways in which we receive and deal with reasons. Accordingly, we might collect them together under the term *reasonableness*; thus, democratic citizens must manifest the capacities of reasonableness.

Democratic citizenship also requires capacities of a different sort. In order to sustain democracy in the face of political losses, citizens must be able to regard each other with a certain kind of *sympathy* or fellow feeling. That is, they must be able to recognize each other as persons who, like themselves, aspire to deploy democratic politics for the sake of their sincerely held values. And they must be able to sustain that sympathy even when they staunchly object to the values that drive their fellow citizens' political views. That is, democratic citizens must have the capacity to recognize that harboring incorrect or even distasteful views about justice and the other great political values does not necessarily disqualify a person for proper democratic citizenship; they must be able to judge that their political opponents are mistaken or misguided without regarding them as therefore unfit for citizenship. We can call this overall capacity democratic *sympathy*.

Certainly there are limits to this requirement. Some conceptions of justice are overtly inconsistent with the fundamental commitments of democratic society. Citizens who embrace views of this kind must be dealt with in various ways, and certain views are not entitled to a hearing or even toleration. There are indeed views the holding of which suffices to render one unfit for citizenship in a democratic society. None of this is being denied here. Still, discussion of the limits of democratic sympathy is beyond our present purview. The point is that there are sharply divided conceptions of fundamental values that, despite their stark opposition to each other, are consistent with proper democratic citizenship. What's distinctive here is that the kind of sympathy called for by democratic citizenship need not involve any muting of such disagreements. The sympathy has as its target one's fellow citizens as earnest moral agents and democratic actors; this is consistent with outright antagonism toward their views.

The account so far has identified two broad capacities—reasonableness and sympathy—that concern relations among democratic citizens. But democratic citizens must cultivate certain self-regarding abilities, too. After all, they must be able to persevere and persist in democratic action despite political losses. In moving forward in the wake of political defeat, they must have patience and ingenuity as well as the ability to exercise prudence. They must be able to plan, strategize, and collaborate with others. They also must be able summon qualities of character that could motivate them to build coalitions, find common cause with others, forge common ground, and coordinate together on plans for democratic action. These capacities can be collectively called *persistence*.

So in order to navigate the dissensus and loss that are inevitable within any political arrangement, citizens must manifest a sufficient degree of reasonableness, sympathy, and persistence. To repeat, democracy is hard. Notice, however, that democracy might not be quite as demanding as it may now seem. The democratic capacities do not require citizens to deny that some of their fellow citizens are cranks, crackpots, or otherwise unscrupulous democratic actors. Nor does this view obligate any citizen to get along with or even talk to anyone in particular. Nothing on offer demands that citizens refrain from sharp political critique or protest of their rivals. And proper democratic citizenship is consistent with the

refusal to engage with certain others who embrace certain political perspectives. Moreover, there is nothing in the account just
sketched that disallows anger and hostility or requires calmness
and politeness among citizens. The democratic capacities that are
being described do not embed the obligation to form communities
or relinquish quarrels. The view rather specifies certain *capacities*
that citizens must cultivate. This is to say that they must be *able to*
regard and treat one another in these ways. In any particular case,
the specific ways in which these capacities manifest behaviorally
depends a great deal on details that we cannot explore here.

Although there is a lot more to say about the democratic
capacities that I have specified, it is not necessary to delve any
deeper into their specifics. Nor does the argument require that we
adopt the rough depiction of these capacities that I have provided.
The account I have presented serves only to establish a general base-
line from which to begin thinking about how democratic citizens
could sustain their democratic commitments in light of political
loss. And the crucial point is simply that democracy can flourish
only when citizens have the capacity to regard each other as *fellow
citizens*, and thus entitled to an equal share of political power, even
amidst ongoing and deep normative conflicts over how political
power should be exercised. Stating this in slightly different terms, if
democracy is to flourish, citizens must be able to treat each other as
equals even when they regard each other as seriously mistaken and
misguided in their political perspective and judgments.

Thus the accounts offered previously of reasonableness, sympathy, and persistence are but one way of understanding the
constituents of a more general disposition that democratic citizens must cultivate. There are alternative ways of characterizing
the distinctively democratic capacities. Nonetheless, it is likely
that any plausible account of these details will be consistent with
the overall argument to follow. What is crucial at present is to acknowledge that democratic citizenship calls for some such profile
of capabilities. In order to set aside debates concerning the precise

nature of the requisite capabilities, it might help to introduce a more general term to capture them. Picking up on the thought that true friendship involves a commitment to another's good despite harboring no illusions regarding his or her flaws, it can be said that democracy requires among citizens a special form of friendship—*civic friendship*.

Civic friendship is different from friendship of the more familiar type. Without provoking longstanding debates among philosophers about the precise nature of friendship, we can say that friendship is a kind of interpersonal relationship, usually involving some degree of face-to-face interaction. Friendship moreover involves certain kinds of care and affection; friends must generally like each other. Friends must also share a set of values, at least to a certain degree. This is because they must feel that the other's good is a component of their own good. Thus, although friendship is consistent with certain kinds of rivalry, friends look after each other and support each other's flourishing.

Things are different with civic friends. Civic friends need not know each other or interact in any direct way. They need not like each other, nor share a sense of each other's good; they needn't see the other's good as a component of their own good. In fact, civic friends might even *dislike* each other as persons. Nonetheless their friendship consists in the mutual respect they show one another in regarding each other as sharers in a social enterprise, entitled to play an equal role in shaping and directing that enterprise. Civic friends thus are able to situate their ongoing and often passionate or even rancorous political opposition within a broader context wherein they remain equal citizens, and thus entitled to an equal share of political power.

It is crucial to recall from the discussion of democratic sympathy that there are limits to what civic friendship demands. Those who embrace political ideals that are inconsistent with the fundamental commitment to self-government among equals are thereby unfit for democratic citizenship, and thus are not entitled to the kind of regard that citizens owe to one another. The question of what *is* owed to them lies outside of our purview. The point at present is simply that there will be a plurality of political views among citizens that are all consistent with the fundamental commitments of a democratic society despite being incompatible (and perhaps inconsistent) with each other. Thus political dissensus and loss are inevitable even among properly democratic citizens. Civic friendship is constituted by the collection of capacities and dispositions that enable citizens to uphold their investment in democracy even in the wake of political losses.

The polarization dynamic smothers and erodes the capacities that are constitutive of civic friendship. To make that point explicit, recall that the polarization dynamic renders us more extreme versions of ourselves, which in turn disables our capacities to hear and reasonably address our critics; this serves to further embed us within likeminded enclaves, which causes us to amplify and exaggerate our differences with our political opponents. Consequently, anyone who is not roughly like ourselves begins to seem alien, radical, unintelligible, and definitely not worth engaging with. Affective political polarization is the result, and as the antipathy intensifies, so too does the sense that our political opponents are incapable of democratic citizenship, and thus unworthy of it.

In undermining civic friendship, then, the polarization dynamic fosters the contrary disposition—*civic enmity*. Civic enmity is different from the forms of antagonism and rancor that are characteristic of a healthy democratic polity. To repeat, the view on offer does not call for a politics without struggle, conflict, and hostility. To the contrary, it has been affirmed that conflict and loss is ineradicable even among a properly democratic citizenry. Civic enmity is rather the disposition to regard one's political opponents and critics as ipso facto unfit for democratic citizenship. It is the view that no degree of deviation from one's own political viewpoint is consistent with proper democracy; thus it involves the position that anyone who holds democratic political power but dissents from one's own political perspective is therefore a threat to democracy itself.

Thus another formulation of our central problem: overdoing democracy activates the polarization dynamic, which promotes civic enmity, and civic enmity undermines democracy. Democracy needs a citizenry of civic friends, but is presently conducted within environments that reliably nurture and inflame civic enmity. This brings us at last to the heart of the challenge posed by overdoing democracy. How can civic friendship be cultivated among civic enemies?

5.4 Correlate Social Goods

To address this question, we must return to a discussion initiated back in Chapter 1 about how it is possible to overdo good things. Recall the distinction drawn there between goods that can be overdone because they are subject to *diminishing marginal utility* and goods that can be overdone by way of *crowding out*. The answer to the question of how civic friendship can be cultivated lies in a thickening of the earlier account of how good things can be overdone.

Let's begin with a point that perhaps will be obvious. There are some goods that are lost in virtue of their being *deliberately* and *directly* pursued. A classic example of a good of this kind is pleasure. Pleasure is a good that is most reliably secured in the pursuit of something else. That is, we *derive* pleasure from endeavors that have something other than pleasure as their aim. When we set out to experience pleasure, when *that* consciously becomes the entire point of our activity, we might enjoy ourselves for a little while, but we eventually wind up dissatisfied. For a similar example, consider fun. It's good to have fun. But the surest way to fail at fun is to make fun the exclusive aim of an activity. When fun becomes the deliberate point of an endeavor, when we act under the description "have fun now," boredom ensues. We seek fun by engaging in activities that have some other objective, and it's in the pursuit of that other goal that we experience fun. Although we certainly can do something *for fun*, we *have fun* while doing something else, where our explicit objective is something other than pursuing fun. Observe the distinctive kind of ennui that prevails among teenagers; they often have nothing to pursue but their own entertainment, and thus lose interest in everything.

We can capture this feature of pleasure and fun by saying that these goods are fundamentally *byproducts*. They arise out of activities that have some other point. We do best to pursue them by an indirect route. Note again that this is not to say that there is no way to do things *for the sake of* fun or pleasure. Indeed, there are lots of activities that we engage in for the sake of these goods. The point rather is that when we do something for the sake of fun, our success depends on having some other goal in mind as the point of the pursuit. For example, we seek to have fun *by playing the game* or *riding the rollercoaster*. One who plays tennis "for fun" must take *playing tennis* to be what she is doing; it is by playing tennis that she has her fun. In general, then, we can intentionally pursue fun or pleasure, but only by pursuing some other end as well.

Something similar can be said about ordinary (as opposed to civic) friendship. Friendship is a good. It's good to have friends. But it's evident that making *friendship* the point of one's interpersonal encounters is a surefire way to alienate people. We make friends by joining with others in collective activities that have some point other than friendship. One could go so far as to say that friendship *emerges* out of shared pursuits and experiences that are not explicitly aimed at creating friendships. This is why friendship withers in the absence of such sharing. Two people might retain the affection and care appropriate for their friendship, but when they share nothing beyond that, they may continue caring for one another but their friendship fades.

This last point indicates that there are some goods that are byproducts in a more complex sense than is at work in the examples of pleasure and fun. Like pleasure and fun, friendship emerges out of activities that have some other objective; it is in the sense a by-product. Yet it is not apt to say that we *derive* friendship from these other endeavors. Unlike fun and pleasure, friendship is not exactly a *product* at all; thus it cannot be a byproduct in any straightforward sense. Friendship rather is an ongoing *joint activity* that involves characteristic dispositions and behaviors of the kind mentioned in the previous section. It stands to reason that its structure should differ from that of fun and pleasure. And indeed it does. Friendship arises from certain collaborative endeavors, and it can be sustained only alongside them. We might say that friendship is a good that can be pursued and nurtured only in the company of certain other pursuits.

To get the flavor of this thought, imagine a friend approaching you with the proposal that you work together on deepening your friendship. This would be a strange proposal, right? But consider that you put that aside and respond, "Sure, let's do that! So what do you propose that we do?" Suppose your friend offers the following nonplussed response, "Huh? I just told you—we're going to deepen our friendship! *That's* what we just agreed to do!" The slightly comical misfire here reveals an important truth about friendship. Friendship is a *correlate good*. That is, its pursuit and flourishing require the pursuit and flourishing of other goods. Friendship can thrive only within a broader horizon of shared goods.

Return once again to Alice. Alice so unreservedly pursues phys-ical fitness that her regimen crowds out all of the other good things she values, including travel and spending time with friends. It was observed earlier that we would have reason to think that Alice's fit-ness project is distorted. She is pursuing the good of fitness at the expense of the activities and experiences that normally supply the point of being fit. Hence we are inclined to characterize Alice's en-deavor with a diagnostic term: she is *obsessed*. And we might even wonder whether this kind of obsession is in the long run even con-sistent with remaining physically fit.

This, too, suggests that the goodness of certain valuable pursuits presupposes a certain degree of breadth and variety in our overall moral lives. So in the absence of flourishing friendships and enriching experiences of the kind that she had once enjoyed while traveling, Alice's flawless physique appears unhealthy and disfigured, perhaps it's even a *symptom*. Again, we tend to regard physical fitness as a good whose value is partly constituted by the other goods that being fit enables one to pursue. Consequently, when fitness is pursued at the *expense* of these other pursuits, it appears deficient and pathological.

Similar thoughts are now available about friendship. We have already noted that friendship is a correlate good; friendship can be pursued and thrive only in the presence of other pursuits. Now it can be added that the good of a friendship is undone when it is one-dimensional or exhaustively fixated on a single other pursuit or aim. This is even more obvious in cases when a purported friendship functions so as to stifle the prospects of the parties involved. The good of friendship has to do in part with the ways in which it *expands* each participant's horizons. Thus it is a commonplace to observe that friends are people whose company we enlist when we seek to try new things. Part of the good of friendship, we might say, is that friends enable new pursuits and hence support one another's growth. The good of friendship is partly constituted by the goods other than friendship that it enables, and there must be a certain breadth and variety to these other goods. And we pursue friendship partly by pursuing with our friends goods of these additional kinds. This is why sharing new pursuits and undertaking new projects together *enriches* a friendship.

Take note of the difference between friends and what are commonly called "buddies." A buddy is a friend-like partner who engages with us in some *particular* kind of activity—fishing, hiking, drinking, clubbing, and so on. It is important to have buddies, but what distinguishes them from friends is that the good of the buddy relation depends on the reliability of parties in supporting and accompanying each other in some limited and often sharply delineated activity. With friends, the good of the relation has to do with the variability of the endeavors that they support and enable. Hence when a friendship no longer involves varied and expanding shared experiences, it stagnates and begins to decline.

Be assured that the account I am developing will not propose that democratic citizens must form friendships or gather together in face-to-face communities. The claim rather is that democratic citizens must cultivate within themselves the dispositions toward one another that are constitutive of *civic* friendship. Civic friendship is different from ordinary friendship in the crucial respects that have already been mentioned. However, the two types of friendship nonetheless have a similar structure.

The capacities that constitute civic friendship are arrested and smothered when relations among citizens are singularly fixated on their civic roles, and thus their allegiances and divisions qua citizens. Like a friendship that is exhaustively fixated on a single activity to the exclusion of all else, civic friendship that is one-dimensionally absorbed by the travails of politics is doomed to instate the polarization dynamic. Thus an earlier slogan: in order for democratic citizens to treat each other properly as citizens, they must be able to regard each other as something more than citizens. We can now add that they must acknowledge each other as equal persons whose lives are devoted to valuable projects and pursuits that lie beyond politics. Pulling these points together, it can be said that when we treat our political opponents *solely* as citizens, we undermine the capacity to regard them as entitled to the political power that they hold; we come instead to understand them as obstacles or threats, not as our equals. Crucially, the same goes for those who share our political allegiances. When our common political aims exhaust the content of our social interactions, we come to regard them as allies and accomplices rather than as fellow citizens. It may sound paradoxical to say so, but when we regard our fellow citizens strictly as citizens, we undercut the capacity to treat them as our equals.

Thus, if we are to cultivate civic friendship, we must find ways to regard each other as something other than—more importantly, something *beyond*—our civic identities and roles. This is more difficult than it might seem. Our social environments are politically saturated. This means that our everyday interactions are largely structured by forces designed to make salient our political allegiances and hence our divisions. This also means that our views about our fellow citizens, especially those who are our political opponents, are largely products of the polarization dynamic and are thus distortions. Accordingly, efforts to initiate cooperation "across the aisle" are insufficient; they depend on the salience of precisely what produces the problem that such efforts are aiming to remedy. From this it follows more clearly that, as democracy depends on civic friendship, democracy can flourish only when politics is put in its place. Our efforts to cultivate civic friendship must begin from encounters and cooperative activities that do not make salient our political profiles and divisions, endeavors in which politics is not merely suppressed or bracketed, but risen above.

5.5 Breaking the Dynamic

I have already conceded that the very idea of a nonpolitical cooperative endeavor is likely to strike us as alien. Consider, though, that this is exactly what we should expect if the diagnostic argument is correct. Under conditions of political saturation, we should have difficulty imagining nonpolitical collective activities. The peculiarity of the very idea is itself a symptom of political saturation and the polarization dynamic. But that is not all. If the argument thus far has been sound, then it is *true* that everything we do together is a manifestation of our politics. That simply is what it means for our social environment to be politically saturated.

In light of this, recall the point from the beginning of this chapter. It would be futile for me to devise a catalogue of nonpolitical cooperative activities. If our social environments are indeed politically saturated and if this saturation has entrenched us in the polarization dynamic, then any example of a nonpolitical endeavor that I might propose is likely to reflect my own political valences and allegiances. And if this much is correct, then taking up any practical proposal I might make is likely only to feed the polarization dynamic. Hence prescribing a catalogue of nonpolitical cooperative activities would be worse than futile; it would be counterproductive. The solution to the problem of overdoing democracy cannot lie in simply taking up some new and out-of-the-ordinary activity with unfamiliar others; any such effort will be freighted with our polarized political personae. Aren't we trapped, then? Maybe not.

There is an understandable tendency to assume that large-scale political problems can be solved only by means of similarly large-scale interventions. Although it is generally warranted, this tendency can mislead us. In some cases, big problems are best addressed by taking small measures. The problem of overdoing democracy is of this latter kind. Its solution emerges from a relatively minor change that we can initiate within ourselves, as individuals.

The problem of overdoing democracy is solved by breaking the polarization dynamic. To achieve this, we need first to bring about within ourselves a *change-in-view* of our political rivals. For reasons already indicated, the required change is not likely to come by way of a "get to know your enemies" strategy; the proposal is not that we must invite our political rivals to lunch, participate in bipartisan softball games, or the like. One is free to engage in these activities, if one wants. But the solution to overdoing democracy ultimately lies *in us* as individuals. More specifically, changing our view of our political opponents requires first a change in how we regard ourselves.

Popular warnings about belief polarization, political polarization, and their varied enabling accompaniments—"echo chambers," "silos," "bubbles," "alternative facts," and so on—most frequently take a *second-personal* or *third-personal* form. That is, when we decry these phenomena, we usually are referring to dysfunctions that have beset others, usually our political rivals. Similarly, when we complain about the state of public discourse in contemporary democracy, we are typically assigning blame to those with whom we disagree. And when we worry about partisan extremism and the intensification of animosity, we almost always are thinking of people politically on the other side. We normally do not regard ourselves as in the grip of the polarization dynamic, and we don't see our political allies as having transformed into more extreme versions of themselves, either. The polarization dynamic appears to us as something that affects other people. We ordinarily cannot recognize it in our own case.

There is a good explanation for this. It would be difficult to sustain our political commitments in the wake of the sincere first-personal assessment that they are products of belief polarization, and thus out of step with our evidence. In other words, *surreptitiousness* is one of the features of the polarization phenomenon; indeed, it is part of the reason why it is widespread. We transform into more extreme versions of ourselves because of forces that are largely imperceptible to us at the time they are taking effect. Accordingly, although we see clearly how polarization has affected our opponents, we tend not to recognize it in ourselves or our allies.

But now that we have identified the mechanisms by which belief polarization operates and the dynamic that it initiates, we have reason to conclude that this asymmetry in assigning its impacts is unfounded. We have reason to acknowledge that the degree to which we regard our opposition as affected by the phenomenon is likely commensurate with the extent to which it has been active in our own case. Indeed, it should be recognized that the tendency to disregard our own vulnerability to the phenomenon is itself a further manifestation of the polarization dynamic; the inclination to see belief polarization at work only in unlike others is yet another mechanism by which we are propelled into further extremity, hived into likeminded clusters, and insulated from the ideas and criticisms of anyone who is not just like us. Thus this tendency is

also a process by which civic friendship is undercut and civic enmity fueled.

So the first step to take toward putting politics in its place is to
acknowledge our own vulnerability to the polarization dynamic.
We need to work to recognize *in ourselves* the vulnerability to the
same distortions and corruptions that we commonly ascribe only
to our political opposition. We should acknowledge that our own
views are likely products of belief polarization. Importantly, the
recommendation is *not* that we each need to rework all of our
political commitments from the ground up. That would be a futile exercise. The more important step is to focus on how we view
our political opponents. Our view of *them* is likely a product of
our own group's depictions; and these are likely driven by certain cohesion dynamics instead of anything that would produce
a nuanced and accurate picture of who they are and what they
believe.

Even though our instincts may say otherwise, our political opposition is not a monolith comprised solely of extremists whose views
threaten the very core of democracy. In fact, some research shows
that over the past thirty years, despite the increasing levels of animosity, rank-and-file members of opposing political parties have
not grown more deeply divided over concrete policies; in fact, on
certain key issues, partisans have moderated, that is, grown less divided.[12] If that strikes you as surprising, recall the Humean dimension of the belief polarization phenomenon. As we become more
intensely committed to our perspective, we come to feel more *affectively* distant from those who do not belong to our own group.
This intensified affective distance produces the sense that we must
be deeply divided over our ideas and thus our views about political
policy. As was already noted, belief polarization produces affective
political polarization, and affective political polarization produces
partisan and platform political polarization. We are all vulnerable
to the polarization dynamic, so we tend to embrace exaggerated
conceptions of the ideological distance between our own political

views and those of our opposition. Those who find that hard to fathom should chalk it up to the polarization dynamic.

It is important to emphasize once again that this point does not require one to adopt a conciliatory stance toward one's political rivals. The claim is not that one needs to moderate one's views regarding policy, or seek to split the difference between one's view and that of one's opposition. Whether this kind of recalibration is called for in light of the symmetry of the polarization dynamic is a distinct question that cannot be engaged here. Recognizing our own vulnerability to the polarization dynamic is not inconsistent with standing firm on our views and sustaining a vigilant program of political action on behalf of our political commitments. The proposal at present is only that one needs to recognize that the common asymmetry in *ascribing* the effects of the polarization dynamic is unfounded, and that one's own view *of one's political opposition* is likely the product of polarization.

This first step might seem easy, involving only a sincere admission of something that has already been well documented. It is a small step; but not all small steps are easy. Our social environments are politically saturated. This means that our social media feeds, our entertainment habits, and much else is aligned with our political profiles, structured to affirm our social identities. The strictly cognitive acknowledgment of the fact that we, too, are vulnerable to polarization does not suffice. To the degree that we are able, we need to try to also engage in positive acts to *mute* the explicitly political corroborations to which we expose ourselves in the ordinary course of daily life. One need not go so far as to delete one's social media accounts; but it might be suggested that one mute or dilute the strictly political accounts that appear in one's feeds, especially those that are fixated on memes that lampoon one's opposition. I will also not claim that one should stop consuming online and cable news; but it should be noted that old-fashioned print and radio have been shown to be more accurate and reliable sources than television news.[13]

The more general point is this. Before one can engage in nonpolitical activities with others, one must take steps to desaturate one's immediate social environment. And so, in addition to unplugging and checking out of the most heavily politically saturated regions of one's social environment, one should also engage in a certain level of restraint and perhaps refusal. For not only do our social environments contain political messaging and other stimuli, they function so as to *extract* overtly political behavior from us. To repeat, putting politics in its place does not require political quietism or resignation; it rather involves the insistence that not every aspect of our social lives that *could* be a site for democratic citizenship therefore *must* be put to that use, and the corresponding resolve to resist the perpetual instigations to commit overt acts of political communication. In other words, putting political in its place involves establishing boundaries within our social environments, and thereby restricting the reach of democracy so that social encounters of other kinds can take place. Hence it is consistent with being a vigilant and conscientious democratic citizen who is fully devoted to justice to simply refuse to use Facebook as a site for political action, for example. And although friends and feeds might contend otherwise, there is no dereliction of one's political duty in using social media strictly to look at videos of pets.

By recognizing our own vulnerability to forces that distort our view of our political opposition, and then taking steps to desaturate our immediate social environments, we begin to break the polarization dynamic. That's a start. It is only after we have made some progress in rehabilitating our view of our political rivals does it make sense to pursue nonpolitical endeavors. Note that the task is not to identify one's political opponents and then propose something to do with them. Nonpolitical cooperative endeavors are not nonpartisan or bipartisan endeavors; that is not the description under which they can be undertaken. Such activities have political cooperation as their explicit aim, and hence they fail to appreciate the way in which civic friendship is a correlate good. The task before us is that of putting politics in its place, and this is done by doing things with others who for all we know might be our political foes; these are endeavors in which politics is simply irrelevant, out of place. In short, we must do something more than attempt to "reach across the aisle." We need also to find sites of cooperation where there's no aisle to reach across.

Recall the earlier example of the friend who proposes that you and he should work together on deepening your friendship. What makes the exchange (mildly) funny is that the friend seems to be confused about the proper description of the activity he is proposing; it is as if he thinks that there is some activity that *intrinsically* deepens friendship. But there is no activity of that kind; whether some activity serves to deepen a friendship depends centrally on the participants. If we are to work on breaking the polarization dynamic, what we need to do is engage in endeavors that satisfy a particular description; namely, they must involve us in cooperative activities with others whose political commitments are not only unknown to us but also beside the point. And although there are certain collective activities that are intrinsically political, whether a collaboration of some other sort counts as nonpolitical in the relevant sense depends largely on *what we bring to it*.

Hence the practical recommendation: after working to rehabilitate your view of your political opponents, try taking up some cooperative project or endeavor that you regard as not having a determinate political valence. If this project is something out of the ordinary for you, all the better. Volunteer to pick up litter in a local park or to teach someone to read at the public library. Sign up with a group that visits the elderly and infirm. Join a bowling team or book club. Register for a cooking class. Participate in a community organization. Begin following a local sports team. Organize a trivia night at a local bar or start up a group that supports local businesses. Audition for a local choir. It ultimately does not matter very much what you choose to try; the important thing is that you do something that you sincerely take not to be an expression of your particular political identity.

Now, if while engaging in this endeavor you find yourself surrounded by others who make salient to you that they share your political profile, try something else. If on the other hand you find yourself surrounded by others who make salient to you that they embrace a political profile that opposes yours, exercise restraint and refusal; make explicit to them that you're not engaging in politics. If that fails, find something else to do. Remember that the goal is to involve yourself in cooperative activities in which politics can simply recede.

That's another small, but not necessarily easy, step. Now notice an additional difficulty: although the prescription is to engage in nonpolitical cooperative activities, these endeavors cannot be exclusively driven by the intention to repair democracy. That is, in joining the bowling league, one must take bowling as central to one's endeavor. Just as someone who plays tennis for fun must describe *playing tennis* as her activity, when one joins a bowling league for the sake of cultivating civic friendship, one must take the central point of the endeavor to be something else, namely *bowling*. Consider someone who joins a bowling league because she wants to make new friends. There is, of course, one sense in which it is correct to say that, in bowling, making new friends is what she's up to. Nonetheless, in order to succeed at making new friends in that way, she must take bowling to be the activity she's engaged in.

The same goes for nonpolitical collaborations aimed at cultivating civic friendship. One may be motivated to engage in them by the desire to contribute to democracy's repair, but the success of that project depends largely on the extent to which one also takes up the interest in the nonpolitical activity *on its own terms*, so to speak. *Cleaning the park, visiting the elderly, contributing to the club, supporting the team*, and so on must be what we take ourselves to be up to, if those activities are likely to cultivate civic friendship. The idea is that if we can multiply social encounters where citizens collaborate to produce what they regard as a valuable outcome, but in collaborating are unaware of one another's political allegiances, we will be on our way to breaking the polarization dynamic as well as cultivating civic friendship.

5.6 Is Civic Friendship Possible?

Let's take stock. I first identified two measures that one can take in order to begin breaking the polarization dynamic and putting politics in its place. The first is to acknowledge one's own vulnerability to polarization; the second is to take small but nonetheless significant steps to desaturate one's immediate environment. I then proposed that once these measures are taken, the next step is to involve oneself in social activities that one sincerely judges are not expressions of one's politics. The overriding objective of these efforts—and the key to breaking the polarization dynamic more generally—is to enable a *rehabilitation* of one's conception of one's political opponents. To acknowledge that our political animosities and divisions are at least partly the result of a debilitating syndrome to which we all are subject is to begin to reestablish the capacity to regard one's political rivals as one's equals. Once we recognize that our perception of the depth and severity of our political divisions are due to a dynamic that afflicts us all, and once we follow that recognition with cooperative engagements that reaffirm the humanity and civility of those whose politics are unknown to us, we can begin to admit that our political conflicts are not necessarily the result of our opposition's depravity and corruption. Hence we will be able to affirm that, despite their being severely misguided, wrong, and ignorant when it comes to the political things that matter most, our political opponents are nonetheless our equals and therefore are entitled to an equal democratic say.

Civic friendship is the capacity to manifest that Janus-faced disposition toward others. Even keeping in mind that the demands of civic friendship apply only among those who embrace political values that are consistent with the democratic ideal, it might seem that civic friendship is impossible. How can we regard those who are by our own lights deeply mistaken about the most important political things as nonetheless entitled to equal power to decide political policy? If, as seems natural to allege, justice is of the utmost importance, then why should we take those whom we regard as mistaken about justice to be our political equals? Is civic friendship even possible?

Civic friendship is frequently conflicted and sometimes distressed, but it is nonetheless possible. Consider an analogy with a familiar and widespread disposition that has a similar structure. On standard accounts, religious toleration is an internally uneasy disposition. It is the capacity to respect another person's conscience while also judging that it has misled that person in a way that is seriously mistaken and perhaps eternally detrimental. To get a firm grip on this, imagine a religiously convicted person holding that (1) there is no salvation outside of my faith; (2) achieving salvation is the most important thing for humans to achieve; and (3) I must do what I am able to help others achieve salvation. Religious toleration involves the additional commitment that (4) it would be wrong, not merely ineffective, for me to employ political force to compel others to engage in the kind of religious observance that is necessary for salvation.

The introduction of this fourth commitment makes for a troubled set. After all, if salvation really is the most important thing for humans to achieve, and if one consequently acknowledges an obligation to assist others in achieving salvation, then what could underwrite the in-principle opposition to deploying force in order to compel the kind of behavior that is necessary for salvation? John Locke notoriously built his case for religious toleration on the premise that compulsion was an *ineffective* means for instilling religious conviction. Here we are explicitly considering a view according to which deployments of force—including political force—would be unjustified even if they would succeed. How could any devout religious believer subscribe to this view?

A slogan commonly espoused by religious believers has it that salvation is too important for politics. The thought is that politics is too petty and crass an instrument for pursuing salvation. Again, it is not that politics is *incapable* of compelling the necessary observances for salvation; rather the idea is that even if force could get the job done, it remains an instrument of the *wrong kind* for that exalted purpose. The stance of the person who is religiously convicted and yet tolerant is nevertheless conflicted. Yet religious toleration is not only widely practiced, but also embraced as a core value within religious communities.

Civic friendship is similar. The civic friend acknowledges others as political equals even though she may also regard them as advocates for injustice and other forms of normative error. How could such a stance be maintained? Again, religious toleration provides a clue. On standard views of the matter, the religiously convicted person is motivated to tolerate the severe theological errors of others by way of an acknowledgment of *conscience*. The tolerant religious believer recognizes even in those who espouse heretical doctrines the exercise of a capacity that she, too, exercises. She regards their error as nevertheless rooted in the noble enterprise of living according to one's own sincere conscience; she thereby comprehends the evil in forcing someone to live against their own conviction. We might say that her toleration is motivated by a respect for that enterprise. So it goes with the civic friend. She regards the political errors of her political opposition as nonetheless rooted in the aspiration to align the political world with one's deepest convictions about justice, freedom, autonomy, and the like. She thereby understands the indignity of being subjected to forms of political coercion that are experienced as brute or merely imposed. And even though she is nonetheless convinced of her own stance concerning these matters, she recognizes and respects in others the enterprise of pursuing a social order that is aligned with one's own conception of justice, so long as that conception is not inconsistent with the fundamental ideal of self-government among equals.

To be sure, civic friendship is demanding. Given its Janus-faced nature, it often manifests in a conflicted stance toward others. But it is no more demanding or distressed than religious toleration, which, to repeat, is both widely practiced and generally valued today. One might say, then, that the problem of overdoing democracy finds the beginning of its solution in the idea of a democratic Reformation. Such a Reformation at once exalts the individual citizen's integrity and civic conscience while also upholding a social ideal of mutual respect.

6

The Place of Politics

Overdoing democracy is democracy's undoing. Yet the tendency to overdo democracy is the stable, predictable result of belief polarization under conditions of political saturation. The trouble with current democratic politics, then, stems from the fact that in contemporary democratic societies, social environments are thoroughly saturated with politics. Thus even our sincere attempts to practice responsible democratic citizenship are plagued by the polarization dynamic; they consequently threaten to intensify and entrench civic enmity. Democratic legitimacy depends on the opposite of civic enmity, civic friendship. Overdoing democracy thus is politically *degenerative*. Democracy overdone is democracy in decline.

Yet we remain a self-governing community of equals. We each have duties as citizens to contribute to our shared democratic order. Hence complete withdrawal from politics is not a responsible option. Putting politics in its place involves the recognition that democratic politics has *its* place, and when we enact our roles as citizens within democracy's site, we are bound to act as vigorously and devotedly as we see fit. But putting politics in its place also involves the recognition that democracy has *a* place, the acknowledgment that democracy is not the all-embracing end and consuming purpose of our social lives. If we are to avoid overdoing democracy while also sustaining responsible levels of democratic engagement, we need to construct sites of cooperative endeavor where politics has no place. This means that we must work to *desaturate* our social environments of politics.

Desaturation can be initiated only by changing ourselves. Specifically, we need to rework our view of our political adversaries. And this alteration begins with turning on ourselves the diagnostic tools we are accustomed to deploying only against others. We must acknowledge that our own favored depictions of our political opponents are products of the polarization dynamic. I emphasize once again that this acknowledgment is consistent with sustaining one's first-order policy commitments; in taking due appreciation of one's vulnerability to the polarization dynamic, one needn't compromise one's assessment of what justice requires, nor must one moderate one's view of the extent to which the other side is wrong. The needed alteration involves only the recognition that the misguidedness of one's political opponents is not necessarily due to degeneracy and corruption. In other words, the required revision involves acknowledging that political error—even of a severe kind—is not always the product of cravenness. We must keep in mind that, as with all of the things that matter most, there is room in politics for reasonable divergence, honest mistakes, blameless fault, and sincere error.

With this internal work done, we can begin to regard our fellow citizens as something more than the political roles they occupy and enact. We next need to find ways to cooperate with others in social contexts where these roles are not salient, and furthermore are beside the point. Given present levels of civic enmity, the resuscitation and cultivation of the capacities that constitute the distinctive components of civic friendship can begin only from within contexts where politics has no place, spaces and endeavors that we can regard as beyond the *reach* of democracy. It is only in acknowledgment of the possibility of social engagements beyond democracy that we can hold politics in its place. And it is only when politics is in its place can our most earnest, energized, and authentic political action positively contribute to the furthering of the democratic ideal.

Formulated most generally, then, the prescription offered in this book is that putting politics in its place requires that we take vigilant measures as individuals to keep mindful of the fact that, even in a democracy, politics isn't the point of *everything* we do together and mustn't be allowed to permeate the whole of our collective lives. Alas, sustaining this recognition is far more difficult than it should be. In addition to the ways in which political saturation operates to obscure this fact, our intuitive understanding of democracy as an ideal prods us in the direction of overextending democracy's reach. Although we are correct to understand democracy as a kind of *society* that is committed to the exalted moral ideal of self-government among equals, it does not follow that the entire horizon of social interaction and interpersonal endeavor is itself a performance of democratic politics. To be sure, some democratic theorists are fond of inflating the idea of democracy to the point that it is identified with whatever political, social, and interpersonal arrangements are best. These views render it a matter of *definition* that democracy cannot be overdone, because *democracy* is the name for the all-encompassing good of humanity. Views employing such a bloated definition serve only to obscure the problems that this book has examined. Thicken the ideal of democracy as much as you please, there are nonetheless things that people living in democratic societies do together that are neither exercises of democratic citizenship nor enactments of democracy. In fact, if the argument of this book has been successful, it follows that there *must be* nonpolitical venues of social engagement.

The *must be* in the previous sentence is both prescriptive and conceptual. It is conceptual in that democratic legitimacy requires citizens to manifest to a sufficient degree the capacities of civic friendship, and civic friendship can take root and thrive only in the presence of nonpolitical shared pursuits. Accordingly, if there could be no such venues because necessarily *everything is politics*, then democratic legitimacy is impossible. I take it that this is a result that democracy's advocates should like to avoid. Furthermore, the *must be* is also prescriptive in that we *need there to be* venues for nonpolitical cooperative endeavor if we are to satisfy our responsibilities as citizens. If we fail to maintain such endeavors, we set ourselves up for failure as democratic citizens, and we thereby implicate ourselves in democracy's decline. Far from a call for emaciated or halfhearted democracy, the proposal is that citizens who are invested in authentic, vibrant, and engaged democracy need to put politics in its place. Democratic politics of that energetic kind can thrive only when it is situated within a broader social environment.

If the thought that politics must be put in its place still raises suspicions, ask yourself what politics is *for*. In asking this question, one is not thereby embracing the idea that democracy's value is strictly instrumental. One can hold that democracy is noninstrumentally valuable while still recognizing that democracy, and political association more generally, is also *for* something. In case this still seems misguided, try rephrasing as follows: What's the *point* of democracy? Why does democracy matter?

On nearly any account, part of democracy's point is that it is necessary (either instrumentally or in some deeper sense) for securing what can be called the *great political values*—justice, equality, liberty, autonomy, dignity, and so on. And although the nature of these great values can also be construed in various ways, it nonetheless makes sense to ask why they matter to the degree that they do. Here the answer is straightforward. These values matter because *human lives* matter. This is not simply to claim that the biological incidence of living human organisms is important; it is rather to say that human lives as *lived biographies* matter. Of course, the question of why lives matter in the cosmic scheme of things is looming; but thankfully that issue can be averted at present. The point is that justice, equality, liberty, autonomy, and dignity matter because it matters to ourselves and to others how our lives go. This is after all why we plan, persevere, struggle, sacrifice, aspire, and strive to *make something* of our lives. Although there is a broad range of defensible but nonetheless opposing conceptions of what it means for a life to go well, there is general consensus that the great political values facilitate our success; they enable us to be the authors of our lives, to make our lives *ours*, to live on our own terms.

Again, whatever kind of value one may assign to democracy in its own right, democracy is also *for* securing and maintaining the conditions under which we can be the authors of our own lives, whatever one might take that to mean. Importantly, embedded within the ideal of democracy is the realization that our lives are irrevocably social; we can make our lives our own only in collaboration with others who are also empowered to live lives of their own making. Living lives of our own involves living in concert with others who are similarly authoring their lives, and this calls for a due recognition of the fact that others are their own authors rather than mere props or the supporting cast in our own biographies. We can capture this thought by saying that the point of democracy is to enable us to live lives devoted to projects and pursuits that manifest valuable human relationships with particular others—relationships of love, care, respect, support, sympathy, appreciation, understanding, and mutuality. Relationships of those kinds are facilitated by conditions under which the great political values are secured and fostered.

To be sure, when understood in this way, democracy is no less rancorous and conflicted. The claim that democracy's point is to enable valuable human relationships does not entail that in a democracy we must all be friends, or that interpersonal hostility and antagonism are incompatible with democracy. Conflict and dissensus are among the ineradicable circumstances of politics. We need a well-structured political order precisely because we can't "*just* get along." As politics inevitably involves exercising power, democracy is always a site of clash and contestation. Thus organizing ourselves politically in a way that is consistent with our status as moral equals takes a great deal of work. Accordingly, acknowledging that the purpose of democracy is to enable valuable human relationships serves as a reminder that the travails and struggles of politics have a point that is important enough to make democracy worth all the effort it requires.

Despite the exhortations of democracy's most ardent enthusiasts, the point of democracy cannot be more and better democracy. And it cannot be the purpose of human life to make democracy flourish. This is because the point of democracy—and also its good—lies in the nurturing of things beyond politics. Although the term is freighted with certain associations that I would disavow, it can be said that the point of politics, and therefore the point of democracy, is human flourishing. *That* is what democracy is for, and I have argued that it is not only confused but also counterproductive to follow those philosophers who simply identify democracy as human flourishing. In overdoing democracy, then, we not only contribute to democracy's dissolution, we also lose track of the point of the entire undertaking. And in losing track of the point of democracy, we render ever more distant the purposes and aspirations that make human life worthwhile. We thereby contribute to the materialization of a collective fate that none of us wants to share.

We are most definitely the kind of creatures that can flourish only amongst others interacting together within an appropriately structured social and political order. As any such order involves exercises of power, our lives are inevitably beset with conflicts over how power should be deployed. Maybe this means that we can live well only under sufficiently democratic arrangements. To be clear, securing, maintaining, and cultivating democracy is a grand and ongoing enterprise that is plausibly regarded as a central component of human flourishing. Nonetheless, our flourishing, both individually and collectively, depends also on the realization of goods that cannot be won by politics alone.

Notes

Introduction

1. This tendency persists. A colleague recently spotted in Nashville a bumper sticker with the message "Trump 2020: Make Liberals Cry Again."
2. Cella 2018.
3. Willingham 2018.
4. Soh 2018.
5. For less recent examples, see Judkis 2016; Bernstein 2016; Post Senning 2016; Miller and Nickalls 2016; Brophy Marcus 2016; Cummings 2017; Pulia 2017; and Obeidallah 2017.
6. Brady et al. 2017.

Chapter 1

1. Addams 1902: 9; Dewey 1927: 325.
2. It should be added that I see no reason to think that the injunction to put politics in its place is conservative in the political sense of that term, either. It is hoped that the view is *consistent* with political conservatism *as well as* progressive (in the United States, "liberal") political platforms.
3. Compare R. Jay Wallace's (2013: 210ff.) analysis of the "bourgeois predicament."
4. Concede for the sake of argument that everything is politics. What, then, can we say *about* politics? What could we say politics is? Once one accepts that everything is politics, anything one says in order to clarify the meaning of the claim must *itself* be understood as politics, too. Suppose, though, that I am trying to find out what politics is, so that I might come to understand what one might mean by saying that everything is politics. It seems my conceptual and explanatory resources have run out. The assertion that everything is politics threatens to render itself unintelligible.
5. Schumpeter 2008: 269. See Przeworski 1999 and Posner 2003 for current versions of this view. A closely related, though not classically minimalist, view can be found in Achen and Bartels 2016.

6. Schumpeter 2008: 283.
7. Schumpeter 2008: 295.
8. Somin 2016 takes this view that smaller government is the best response to widespread public ignorance; Brennan 2016 defends a similar view, though his is not a view about the size of government, but the extent of popular political power.

Chapter 2

1. See Bates 1993 for an account of the legal case and Macedo 2000 for a treatment of the philosophical issues it raises.
2. Lynch 2014: 6.
3. Rousseau 1988: 92.
4. Estlund 2000; Mulligan 2018.
5. Lopez-Guerra 2011; Landemore 2012; Guerrero 2014.
6. See Pateman 1970; Mansbridge 1983; and Barber 2004.
7. Putnam 1995.
8. Goodin 2000: 92.
9. Young 1996.
10. Cohen 1989.
11. Pettit 2012: 225.
12. Gutmann and Thompson 2004: 80.
13. Sunstein 2017.
14. Gastil 2008; Fishkin 2009.
15. Ackerman and Fishkin 2004; Leib 2004.

Chapter 3

1. On this, see Jennings and Stoker 2016.
2. See Rohrschneider and Whitefield 2009, and Schmitt and Freire 2012.
3. Pew 2014a.
4. Pew 2016. See also Taylor 2016a and Taylor 2016b.
5. For skepticism, see Fiorina, Abrams, and Pope 2005. For other book-length treatments, see Levendusky 2009; Campbell 2016; and Mason 2018. For helpful overviews, see Hetherington 2009; Mason 2015; and Johnston, Manley, and Jones 2016.
6. See Lelkes 2016.
7. Sunstein 2015.

8. Thaler and Sunstein 2008; Thaler and Sunstein 2003.

9. This position is defended in Lanier 2018.

10. Thus Bishop (2009: 40), "The country may be more diverse than ever coast to coast. But look around: our streets are filled with people who live alike, think alike, and vote alike."

11. Chen and Rodden 2013. See also Tam Cho, Gimpel, and Hui 2013.

12. Iyengar and Krupenkin 2018. See also Williamson 2008.

13. For one example, see Aristotle 1992: VIII.1.

14. Bogardus 1925. See also the first chapter of Mason 2018 for a discussion of the relevant sociological literature.

15. Cahn and Carbone 2010; Pew 2014a: 42–50; Taylor 2016b: 7–9.

16. Tapestry: http://www.esri.com/data/tapestry/zip-lookup. This site is free to use, but it is also a promotional vehicle for additional Esri products that provide even more detailed lifestyle data about regional populations.

17. https://teleport.org/about-us/

18. Lafrance 2014.

19. Williamson 2008.

20. Margolis 2018.

21. Skocpol 2013: 212–220.

22. Mutz and Mondak 2006.

23. Gift and Gift 2015.

24. Bonica, Chilton, and Sen 2015.

25. Carney, Jost, Gosling, and Potter 2008.

26. Iyengar 2016.

27. Pew 2014a: 48. Iyengar and Westwood 2015: 691–692.

28. Iyengar and Westwood 2015: 692. See also Huber and Malhotra 2017; and Klofstad, McDermott, and Hatemi 2012.

29. Huber and Malhotra 2017: 278–280.

30. Arfer and Jones 2019. Interestingly this study finds a *positive* correlation between conservative political affiliation and use of the Ashley Madison website. And Democrats were found to be the most infrequent users of the site.

31. Nicholson, Coe, Emory, and Song 2016.

32. Iyengar and Konitzer 2017: 24.

33. Bishop 2009: 255. Compare Iyengar (2016: 220), "Today, Republicans and Democrats differ not only in their politics, but also in terms of their ethnic, religious, and regional identities"; and Mason (2018: 13), "Democrats and Republicans have become different types of people." See also Shi, Mast, Weber, Kellum, and Macy 2017.

34. Mason and Wronski 2018: 257.

35. Cf. Bennett 1998.
36. See Hetherington and Weiler 2018 for some current data.
37. For a sampling, see Wilson 2013; Wilson 2014; Weber 2013; and Maheshwari 2018.
38. McConnell, Margalit, Halhorta, and Levendusky 2017: 12–13. See also Gerber and Huber 2009.
39. Bishop 2009: 184.
40. See, for example, Sunstein 2017 and Mutz 2015.
41. See Peterson, Goel, and Iyengar 2017.
42. It is worth noting that currently MSNBC is using the slogan "This is Who We Are" in advertisements for its programming.
43. See, for example, the 2004 PIPA report on "The Separate Realities of Bush and Kerry Supporters." See also Kull, Ramsay, and Lewis 2013.
44. Pew 2014b: 1.
45. This has been a major theme of Sunstein's work for more than two decades. For the most current treatment, see Sunstein 2017.
46. Sunstein 2017: 154–256.
47. Pew 2016.
48. Iyengar, Sood, and Lelkes 2012: 408.
49. Miller and Conover 2015.
50. Claussen and Ensley 2016.
51. Iyengar and Westwood 2015.
52. Pew 2014a: 35.
53. As I type this sentence, I am reminded that #SecondCivilWar is currently trending on social media. The alt-right conspiracy monger Alex Jones promoted on his website the claim that Democrats were planning to declare war on their fellow citizens on July 4, 2018. This of course did not happen, and Jones was subjected to a mocking campaign on social media with its own hashtag (#SecondCivilWarLetters).
54. Coffey and Joseph 2013: 133; Iyengar and Westwood 2015: 691; and Margolis and Sances 2017.
55. Carney, Jost, Gosling, and Potter 2008: 835.
56. Shah, McLeod, Kim, Lee, Gotlieb, Ho, and Breivik 2007: 219.
57. Mason 2018: 44.
58. Coffey and Joseph 2013: 118.
59. Shah, McLeod, Kim, Lee, Gotlieb, Ho, and Breivik 2007.
60. See Stolle and Micheletti 2013 for a full treatment.
61. Coffey and Joseph 2013: 118.
62. Neither does the NRA online store.

Chapter 4

1. Pew 2016: 3.
2. Pew 2016: 8.
3. For a sample of the genre, see Kruse and Zelizer 2019; Chua 2018; Schneider 2018; Levitsky and Ziblatt 2018; Rosenfeld 2017; and Taylor 2016b.
4. The nomenclature here is tricky. What I'm calling belief polarization is generally known as *group polarization*. Though it is the more common term, I find "group polarization" misleading in the current context, mainly because what I have just described as *political polarization* concerns groups, and the contrasting phenomenon has to do with the beliefs of group members. Still, the terms are not entirely satisfactory. Note that the term *belief polarization* is used by some epistemologists to characterize cases where in the course of a disagreement, interlocutors become more dogmatic. For this use, see Kelly 2008. My use of the term differs from Kelly's. To add an additional complication, in the course of my argument it will become clear that what I'm calling *belief polarization* isn't strictly about beliefs. Alas, sorting out the terminological mess lies far beyond my present objectives.
5. Mason 2018: 60ff.
6. It is so common, in fact, that researchers in 1978 declared that "seldom in the history of social psychology has a nonobvious phenomenon been so firmly grounded in data from across a variety of cultures and dependent measures" (Lamm and Myers 1978: 146). Since that time, the documentation of belief polarization has only further accumulated. The appendix of Sunstein 2009 provides summaries of some of the most important experimental findings.
7. Sunstein 2009: 18–19. Baron, Hoppe, Kao, Brunsman, Linneweh, and Rogers 1996.
8. Moscovici and Zavalloni 1969.
9. Myers and Bishop 1970: 778–779.
10. Myers 1975.
11. Hastie, Schkade, and Sunstein 2007. My account here follows the summary in Sunstein 2009: 5–8.
12. In fact, the phenomenon known as "risky shift," when a group's post-discussion likeliness to engage in risky collective behavior exceeds any of its individual member's pre-discussion willingness to endorse that level of risk for the group, is generally understood to be a special manifestation of belief polarization. See Isenberg 1986: 1141. See also the catalogue of "unfortunate events that have been blamed on group polarization" provided in

Sia, Tan, and Wei 2002: 71–72. These include the Johnson administration's decision to escalate the Vietnam War, the risk-taking at NASA that arguably led to the Challenger explosion, and certain failing trends in finance.

13. Schkade, Sunstein, and Kahneman 2000.

14. Johnson, Stemler, and Hunter 1977.

15. We cannot engage the issue here, but note that there is an ongoing dispute among philosophers concerning how degree of belief is best understood. One influential suggestion, proposed by Frank Ramsey (1990), is that degree of belief can be measured by the believer's *willingness to bet* a substantial sum of money on the belief's truth—a higher degree of belief is suggested by a willingness to bet a larger sum of money on the belief's truth.

16. Burnstein and Vinokur 1977.

17. Sunstein 2017: 72.

18. Myers, Bruggink, Kersting, and Schlosser 1980. See also Zajonc 1968.

19. Sunstein 2009: 40–42.

20. Van Swol 2009: 194.

21. Vinokur and Burnstein 1978.

22. Lamm and Myers 1978: 185.

23. Abrams, Wetherell, Cochrane, Hogg, and Turner 1990.

24. Le 2007.

25. Abrams, Wetherell, Cochrane, Hogg, and Turner 1990. Note also that individuals who have been belief polarized may also be prone to the "backfire effect"; when a belief they hold on the basis of their group identity is contradicted by someone perceived to be outside the relevant group, their confidence in the challenged belief intensifies—they come to hold the belief even more ardently. On this, see Nyhan and Reifler 2010 and Munro and Ditto 1997. But there is a debate regarding the robustness of this phenomenon; see Haglin 2017 and Wood and Porter 2019.

26. I follow the account in Baron, Hoppe, Kao, Brunsman, Linneweh, and Rogers 1996.

27. I set aside cases where a large number of instances of corroboration might *itself* constitute a kind of evidence.

28. Baron, Hoppe, Kao, Brunsman, Linneweh, and Rogers 1996: 558–559.

29. Sunstein 2009: 29.

30. Baron, Hoppe, Kao, Brunsman, Linneweh, and Rogers 1996: 559.

31. Baron, Hoppe, Kao, Brunsman, Linneweh, and Rogers 1996: 559.

32. Sunstein 2009: 24. See also Pariser 2011 and Vaidhyanathan 2018.

33. Del Vicario, Vivaldo, Bessi, Zollo, Scala, Caldarelli, and Quattrociocchi 2016; see also Garimella and Weber 2017.

34. I invoke Hume's name with some trepidation. To be clear, my contention is not that this is a view that David Hume affirmed. Neither am I contending that it is a view that he *would have* embraced. In calling the view *Humean*, I mean only to highlight that the extremity-shift is initiated by a certain kind of affective change in the subject: the increase in our feeling of self-confidence leads to a shift to a more extreme belief content. I hold that this account fits nicely with Hume's general conceptions of belief acquisition and belief change, but this demonstration cannot be attempted here.

35. Westfall, Van Boven, Chambers, and Judd 2015.

36. Iyengar and Krupenkin 2018.

37. Pew 2016: 5.

38. Marks, Copland, Loh, Sunstein, and Sharot 2018.

39. MacIntyre 1984: 254.

40. Dewey 1939: 367–368.

Chapter 5

1. For a summary statement along these lines, as well as citations to documenting literature, see Curato, Dryzek, Ercan, Hendricks, and Niemeyer 2017. Fishkin 2018 is an extended argument for this view.

2. Ackerman and Fishkin 2004; E. Leib 2004.

3. Christopher Karpowitz and Chad Raphael 2014; Grönlund, Bächtiger, and Setälä, eds. 2014.

4. Sunstein 2017: 226.

5. See, for example, Bail et al. 2018.

6. Mutz 2006.

7. Mutz 2006: 75.

8. For example, see Neblo et al. 2010.

9. For example, Curato et al. (2017: 33) claims that "deliberation is the solution to [belief] polarization," but then offers as evidence that "polarization is not found" in properly deliberative groups.

10. Curato et al. 2017: 33.

11. Sunstein 2017: 91.

12. Fiorina, Abrams, and Pope 2005; Fiorina, Abrams, and Pope 2008.

13. Kull, Ramsay, and Lewis 2013.

Works Cited

Abrams, D., M. Wetherell, S. Cochrane, M. A. Hogg, and J. C. Turner. 1990. "Knowing What to Think by Knowing Who You Are: Self-categorization and the Nature of Norm Formation, Conformity and Group Polarization." *British Journal of Social Psychology* 29.2: 97–119.

Achen, Christopher H. and Larry M. Bartels. 2016. *Democracy for Realists: Why Elections Do Not Produce Responsive Government*. Princeton, NJ: Princeton University Press.

Ackerman, Bruce and James S. Fishkin. 2004. *Deliberation Day*. New Haven, CT: Yale University Press.

Addams, Jane. 1902. *Democracy and Social Ethics*. London: Macmillan.

Arfer, Kodi B. and Jason J. Jones. 2019. "American Political-Party Affiliation as a Predictor of Usage of an Adultery Website." *Archives of Sexual Behavior* 48.3: 715–723.

Aristotle. 1992. *The Nichomachean Ethics*. David Ross, trans. New York: Oxford University Press.

Bail, Christopher A., Lisa P. Argyle, Taylor W. Brown, John P. Bumpus, Haohan Chen, M. B. Fallin Hunzaker, Jaemin Lee, Marcus Mann, Friedolin Merhout, and Alexander Volfovsky. 2018. "Exposure to Opposing Views on Social Media Can Increase Political Polarization." *Proceedings of the National Academy of Sciences* 115.37: 9216–9221.

Baron, Robert S., Sieg I. Hoppe, Chaun Feng Kao, Bethany Brunsman, Barbara Linneweh, and Diana Rogers. 1996. "Social Corroboration and Opinion Extremity." *Journal of Experimental Social Psychology* 32.6: 537–560.

Barber, Benjamin R. 2004. *Strong Democracy: Participatory Politics for a New Age*. Los Angeles: University of California Press.

Bates, Stephen. 1993. *Battleground*. New York: Poseidon Books.

Bennett, Lance W. 1998. "The UnCivic Culture: Communication, Identity, and the Rise of Lifestyle Politics." *PS: Political Science & Politics* 31.4: 755.

Bernstein, Elizabeth. 2016. "How to Have Thanksgiving Dinner Without a Family Blowup," *Wall Street Journal*. November 20. https://www.wsj.com/articles/how-to-have-thanksgiving-dinner-without-a-family-blowup-1479643202.

Bishop, Bill. 2009. *The Big Short: Why the Clustering of Like-Minded America Is Tearing Us Apart*. New York: Harcourt Publishing Co.

Bogardus, Emory S. 1925. "Social Distance and Its Origins." *Journal of Applied Sociology* 9: 216–226.

Bonica, Adam, Adam Chilton, and Maya Sen. 2015. "The Political Ideologies of American Lawyers." *Journal of Legal Analysis* 8.2: 292–294.

Brady, William J., Julian A. Wills, John Jost, Joshua Tucker, and Jay Van Bavel. 2017. "Emotion Shapes the Diffusion of Moralized Content in Social Networks." *Proceedings of the National Academy of Sciences* 114.28: 7313–7318.

Brennan, Jason. 2016. *Against Democracy.* Princeton, NJ: Princeton University Press.

Brophy Marcus, Mary. 2016. "The politics of Thanksgiving: Keeping the peace post-election," *CBS News.* November 22. https://www.cbsnews.com/news/thanksgiving-politics-keeping-the-peace-with-family-post-election-donald-trump-hillary-clinton/.

Burnstein, Eugene and Amiram Vinokur. 1977. "Persuasive Argumentation and Social Comparison as Determinants of Attitude Polarization." *Journal of Experimental Social Psychology* 13: 315–332.

Cahn, Naome and June Carbone. 2010. *Red Families v. Blue Families: Legal Polarization and the Creation of Culture.* New York: Oxford University Press.

Campbell, James E. 2016. *Polarized: Making Sense of Divided America.* Princeton, NJ: Princeton University Press.

Carney, Dana R., John T. Jost, Samuel D. Gosling, and Jeff Potter. 2008. "The Secret Lives of Liberals and Conservatives: Personality Profiles, Interaction Styles, and the Things They Leave Behind." *Political Psychology* 29.6: 807–840.

Cella, Mary. 2018. "Safe Topics to Discuss This Holiday Season," *New York Times.* November 17. https://www.nytimes.com/2018/11/17/opinion/sunday/thanksgiving- family-political-discussion.html.

Chen, Jowei and Jonathan Rodden. 2013. "Unintentional Gerrymandering: Political Geography and Electoral Bias in Legislatures." *Quarterly Journal of Political Science* 8.3: 239–269.

Chua, Amy. 2018. *Political Tribes: Group Instinct and the Fate of Nations.* New York: Penguin.

Claassen, Ryan L. and Michael Ensley. 2016. "Motivated Reasoning and Yard-Sign Stealing Partisans: Mine Is a Likeable Rogue, Yours Is a Degenerate Criminal." *Political Behavior* 38: 317–335.

Coffey, Daniel J. and Patricia Hallam Joseph. 2013. "A Polarized Environment: The Effect of Partisanship and Ideological Values on Individual Recycling and Conservation Behavior." *American Behavioral Sciences* 57.1: 133.

Cohen, Joshua. 1989. "Deliberation and Democratic Legitimacy." In *The Good Polity*, eds. A. Hamlin and P. Pettit, 17–34. Oxford: Blackwell.

Cummings, William. 2017. "Trump's in the White House, turkey's on the table: What to do if you don't want to talk politics," *USA Today.* November 17. https://www.usatoday.com/story/news/nation/2017/11/17/trump-era-holiday-survival-guide/864764001/.

Curato, Nicole, John S. Dryzek, Selen A. Ercan, Carolyn M. Hendricks, and Simon Niemeyer. 2017. "Twelve Key Findings in Deliberative Democracy Research." *Daedalus* 146.3: 28–38.

Del Vicario, Michela, Gianna Vivaldo, Alessandro Bessi, Fabiana Zollo, Antonio Scala, Guido Caldarelli, and Walter Quattrociocchi. 2016. "Echo Chambers: Emotional Contagion and Group Polarization on Facebook." *Scientific Reports* 6.1: 1–14.

Dewey, John. 1927. *The Public and Its Problems*. In *The Later Works of John Dewey* Vol. 2 (1925–1927). Ed. Jo Ann Boydston. Carbondale: Southern Illinois University Press.

Dewey, John. 1939. "Democratic Ends Need Democratic Methods for Their Realization." In *The Later Works of John Dewey* Vol. 14 (1925–1953). Ed. Jo Ann Boydston. Carbondale: Southern Illinois University Press.

Estlund, David. 2000. "Political Quality." *Social Philosophy and Policy* 17.1: 127–160.

Fiorina, Morris P., Samuel J. Abrams, and Jeremy C. Pope. 2005. *Culture War? The Myth of a Polarized America*. London: Pearson Longman.

Fiorina, Morris P., Samuel J. Abrams, and Jeremy C. Pope. 2008. "Polarization in the American Public: Misconceptions and Misreadings." *Journal of Politics* 70.2: 556–560.

Fishkin, James S. 2009. *When the People Speak: Deliberative Democracy and Public Consultation*. New York: Oxford University Press.

Fishkin, James S. 2018. *Democracy When the People Are Thinking*. New York: Oxford University Press.

Garimella, Venkata and Ingmar Weber. 2017. "A Long-Term Analysis of Polarization on Twitter." *Proceedings of the Eleventh International AAAI Conference on Web and Social Media*: 528–531.

Gastil, John. 2008. *Political Communication and Deliberation*. Thousand Oaks, CA: Sage Publications Inc.

Gerber, Alan S. and Gregory A. Huber. 2009. "Partisanship and Economic Behavior: Do Partisan Differences in Economic Forecasts Predict Real Economic Behavior?" *American Political Science Review* 103.3: 407–426.

Gift, K. and T. Gift. 2015. "Does Politics Influence Hiring? Evidence from a Randomized Experiment." *Political Behavior* 37.2: 653–675.

Goodin, Robert. 2000. "Democratic Deliberation Within." *Philosophy and Public Affairs* 29.1: 81–109.

Grönlund, Kimmo, André Bächtiger, and Maija Setälä, eds. 2014. *Deliberative Mini-Publics: Involving Citizens in the Democratic Process*. Colchester, UK: ECPR Press.

Guerrero, Alexander. 2014. "Against Elections: The Lottocratic Alternative." *Philosophy and Public Affairs* 42: 135–178.

Gutmann, Amy and Dennis Thompson. 2004. *Why Deliberative Democracy?* Princeton, NJ: Princeton University Press.

Haglin, Kathryn. 2017. "The Limitations of the Backfire Effect." *Research and Politics*, July–September: 1–5.

Hastie, Reid, David Schkade, and Cass R. Sunstein. 2007. "What Happened on Deliberation Day?" *California Law Review* 95.3: 915–940.

Hetherington, Marc J. 2009. "Putting Polarization in Perspective." *British Journal of Political Science* 39.2: 413–448.

Hetherington, Marc and Jonathan Weiler. 2018. *Prius or Pickup?* Boston: Houghton Mifflin Harcourt.

Huber, Gregory A. and Neil Malhotra. 2017. "Political Homophily in Social Relationships: Evidence from Online Dating Behavior." *Journal of Politics* 79.1: 269–283.

Isenberg, Daniel J. 1986. "Group Polarization: A Critical Review and Meta-Analysis." *Journal of Personality and Social Psychology* 50.6: 1141–1151.

Iyengar, Shanto and Masha Krupenkin. 2018. "The Strengthening of Partisan Affect." *Advances in Political Psychology* 39.1: 201–218.

Iyengar, Shanto. 2016. "*E Pluribus Pluribus*, or Divided We Stand." *Public Opinion Quarterly* 80, Special Issue: 219–224.

Iyengar, Shanto and Sean J. Westwood. 2015. "Fear and Loathing Across Party Lines: New Evidence on Group Polarization." *American Journal of Political Science* 59.3: 690–707.

Iyengar, Shanto and Tobias Konitzer. 2017. "The Moderating Effects of Marriage Across Party Lines." Working paper. https://pdfs.semanticscholar.org/a55b/50f3de44529ee301c662aa42fb244e4ab992.pdf.

Iyengar, Shanto, Guarav Sood, and Yphach Lelkes. 2012. "Affect, Not Ideology: A Social Identity Perspective on Polarization." *Public Opinion Quarterly* 76.2: 405–431.

Jennings, Will and Gerry Stoker. 2016. "The Bifurcation of Politics: Two Englands." *Political Quarterly* 87.3: 372–382.

Johnson, Norris R., James G. Stemler, and Deborah Hunter. 1977. "Crowd Behavior as 'Risky Shift': A Laboratory Experiment." *Sociometry* 40.2: 183–187.

Johnston, Ron, David Manley, and Kelvyn Jones. 2016. "Spatial Polarization of Presidential Voting in the United States, 1992–2012: The 'Big Sort' Revisited." *Annals of the American Association of Geographers* 106.5: 1047–1062.

Judkis, Maura. 2016. "Fight, flight or drink: Surviving Thanksgiving when you hate how your family voted," *Washington Post*. November 18. https://www.washingtonpost.com/news/food/wp/2016/11/18/fight-flight-or-drink-surviving-thanksgiving-when-you-hate-how-your-family-voted/?noredirect=on&utm_term=.7837ede1b948.

Karpowitz, Christopher and Chad Raphael. 2014. *Deliberation, Democracy, and Civic Forums: Improving Equality and Publicity*. Cambridge, UK: Cambridge University Press.

Kelly, Thomas. 2008. "Disagreement, Dogmatism, and Belief Polarization." *Journal of Philosophy* 105.10: 611–633.

Klofstad, Casey A., Rose McDermott, and Peter K. Hatemi. 2012. "The Dating Preferences of Liberals and Conservatives." *Political Behavior* 35: 519–538.

Kruse, Kevin M. and Julian E. Zelizer. 2019. *Fault Lines: A History of the United States since 1974*. New York: W. W. Norton.

Kull, Steven, Clay Ramsay, and Evan Lewis. 2013. "Misperceptions, the Media, and the Iraq War." *Political Science Quarterly* 118.4: 569–598.

Lafrance, Adrienne. 2014. "Big Data Can Guess Who You Are Based on Your Zip Code," *Atlantic Monthly*. October 14.

Lamm, Helmut and David Myers. 1978. "Group-Induced Polarization of Attitudes and Behavior." *Advances in Experimental Social Psychology* 11: 145–187.

Landemore, Hélène. 2012. *Democratic Reason: Politics, Collective Intelligence, and the Rule of the Many*. Princeton, NJ: Princeton University Press.

Lanier, Jaron. 2018. *Ten Arguments for Deleting Your Social Media Accounts Right Now*. New York: Henry Holt and Company.

Le, Eun-Ju. 2007. "Deindividuation Effects on Group Polarization in Computer-Mediated Communication: The Role of Group Identification, Public-Self-Awareness, and Perceived Argument Quality." *Journal of Communication* 57.2: 385–403.

Leib, Ethan J. 2004. *Deliberative Democracy in America: A Proposal for a Popular Branch of Government*. University Park: Pennsylvania State University Press.

Lelkes, Yphtach. 2016. "Mass Polarization: Manifestations and Measurements." *Public Opinion Quarterly* 80, Special Issue: 392–410.

Levendusky, Matthew. 2009. *The Partisan Sort: How Liberals Became Democrats and Conservatives Became Republicans*. Chicago: University of Chicago Press.

Levitsky, Steven and Daniel Ziblatt. 2018. *How Democracies Die*. New York: Crown Publishing Group.

Lopez-Guerra, Claudio. 2011. "The Enfranchisement Lottery." *Politics, Philosophy, and Economics* 10.2: 211–233.

Lynch, Michael P. 2014. *In Praise of Reason*. Cambridge, MA: MIT Press.

MacIntyre, Alasdair. 1984. *After Virtue: A Study in Moral Theory*. Notre Dame, IN: University of Notre Dame Press.

Macedo, Stephen. 2000. *Diversity and Distrust*. Cambridge, MA: Harvard University Press.

Maheshwari, Sapna. 2018. "When Is a Burrito More than Just a Burrito? When It's a Lifestyle," *New York Times*. July 29. https://www.nytimes.com/2018/07/29/business/media/lifestyle-brands-marketing.html.

Mansbridge, Jane J. 1983. *Beyond Adversary Democracy*. Chicago: University of Chicago Press.

Margolis, Michele F. 2018. *From Politics to the Pews*. Chicago: University of Chicago Press.

Margolis, Michele F. and Michael W. Sances. 2017. "Partisan Differences in Nonpartisan Activity: The Case of Charitable Giving." *Political Behavior* 39: 1–26.

Marks, Joseph, Eloise Copland, Eleanor Loh, Cass Sunstein, and Tali Sharot. 2018. "Epistemic Spillovers: Learning Others' Political Views Reduces the Ability to Assess and Use Their Expertise in Nonpolitical Domains." Harvard Public Law working paper. https://papers.ssrn.com/sol3/papers. cfm?abstract_id=3162009.

Mason, Lilliana. 2015. "'I Disrespectfully Agree': The Differential Effects of Partisan Sorting on Social and Issue Polarization." *American Journal of Political Science* 59.1: 128–145.

Mason, Lilliana. 2018. *Uncivil Agreement: How Politics Became Our Identity*. Chicago: University of Chicago Press.

Mason, Lilliana and Julie Wronski. 2018. "One Tribe to Bind Them All: How Our Social Group Attachments Strengthen Partisanship." *Advances in Political Psychology* 39.1: 257–277.

McConnell, Christopher, Yotam Margalit, Neil Halhorta, and Matthew Levendusky. 2017. "The Economic Consequences of Partisanship in a Polarized Era." *American Journal of Political Science* 62.1: 5–18.

Miller, Patrick R. and Pamela Johnston Conover. 2015. "Red and Blue States of Mind: Partisan Hostility and Voting in the United States." *Political Research Quarterly* 68.2: 225–239.

Miller, Matt and Sammy Nickalls. 2016. "How to Talk Politics Over the Holidays Without Being a Dick," *Esquire*. November 22. https://www.esquire.com/news-politics/news/a50899/talking-politics-thanksgiving/.

Moscovici, S. and M. Zavalloni. 1969. "The Group as a Polarizer of Attitudes." *Journal of Personality and Social Psychology* 12.2: 125–135.

Mulligan, Thomas. 2018. "Plural Voting for the Twenty-First Century." *Philosophical Quarterly* 68.271: 286–306.

Munro, Geoffrey D. and Peter H. Ditto. 1997. "Biased Assimilation, Attitude Polarization, and Affect in Reactions to Stereotype-Relevant Scientific Information." *Personality and Social Psychology Bulletin* 23.6: 636–653.

Mutz, Diana. 2006. *Hearing the Other Side: Deliberative versus Participatory Democracy*. Cambridge UK: Cambridge University Press.

Mutz, Diana. 2015. *In Your Face Politics: The Consequences of Uncivil Media*. Princeton, NJ: Princeton University Press.

Mutz, Diana C. and Jeffrey J. Mondak. 2006. "The Workplace as a Context for Cross-Cutting Political Discourse." *Journal of Politics* 68.1: 140–155.

Myers, D. G. 1975. "Discussion-Induced Attitude Polarization." *Human Relations* 28.8: 699–714.

Myers, D. G. and G. D. Bishop. 1970. "Discussion Effects on Racial Attitudes." *Science* 169.3947: 778–779.

Myers, D. G., J. B. Bruggink. R. C. Kersting, and B. A. Schlosser. 1980. "Does Learning Others' Opinions Change One's Opinion?" *Personality and Social Psychology Bulletin* 6: 253–260.

Neblo, Michael, Kevin M. Esterling, Ryan P. Kennedy, David M. J. Lazer, and Anana E. Sokhey. 2010. "Who Wants to Deliberate—And Why?" *American Political Science Review* 104.3: 566–583.

Nicholson, Stephen P., Chelsea M. Coe, Jason Emory, and Anna V. Song. 2016. "The Politics of Beauty: The Effects of Partisan Bias on Physical Attractiveness." *Political Behavior* 38.4: 883–898.

Nyhan, Brendan and Jason Reifler. 2010. "When Corrections Fail: The Persistence of Political Misperceptions." *Political Behavior* 32.2: 303–330.

Obeidallah, Dean. 2017. "A Guide to Surviving the First Trumpsgiving," *Daily Beast.* November 23. https://www.thedailybeast.com/a-guide-to-surviving-the-first-trumpsgiving.

Pariser, Eli. 2011. *The Filter Bubble: What the Internet Is Hiding from You.* New York: Penguin.

Pateman, Carole. 1970. *Participation and Democratic Theory.* Cambridge, UK: Cambridge University Press.

Peterson, Erik, Sharad Goel, and Shanto Iyengar. 2017. "Echo Chambers and Partisan Polarization: Evidence from the 2016 Presidential Campaign." Working paper. https://5harad.com/papers/selective-exposure.pdf.

Pettit, Phillip. 2012. *On the People's Terms: A Republican Theory and Model of Democracy.* Cambridge, UK: Cambridge University Press.

Pew Research Center. 2014a. "Political Polarization in the American Public." June 12. http://www.people-press.org/2014/06/12/political-polarization-in-the-american-public/.

Pew Research Center. 2016. "Partisanship and Political Animosity in 2016." June 22. http://www.people-press.org/2016/06/22/partisanship-and-political-animosity-in-2016/.

Pew Research Center. 2014b. "Political Polarization and Media Habits" October 21. https://www.pewresearch.org/wp-content/uploads/sites/8/2014/10/Political-Polarization-and-Media-Habits-FINAL-REPORT-7-27-15.pdf.

Posner, Richard A. 2003. *Law, Pragmatism, and Democracy.* Cambridge, MA: Harvard University Press.

Post Senning, Daniel. 2016. "How to Avoid Politics and Survive Your Thanksgiving Meal," *Fortune.* November 24. http://fortune.com/2016/11/24/donald-trump-thanksgiving-politics/.

Program on International Policy Attitudes (PIPA). 2004. "The Separate Realities of Bush and Kerry Supporters." October 21. https://drum.lib.umd.edu/bitstream/handle/1903/10533/The%20Separate%20Realities%20of%20Bush%20and%20Kerry%20Supporters.pdf?sequence=3&isAllowed=y.

Przeworski, Adam. 1999. "Minimalist Conceptions of Democracy: A Defense." In *Democracy's Value*, eds. Ian Shapiro and Casiano Hacker-Cordón, 23–55. Cambridge, UK: Cambridge University Press.

Pulia, Shalayne. 2017. "How to Survive the Holidays When Your Relatives Are Trump Supporters," *In Style*. November 22. https://www.instyle.com/holidays-occasions/how-to-survive-holidays-relatives-trump-supporters.

Putnam, Robert D. 1995. "Bowling Alone: America's Declining Social Capital." *Journal of Democracy* 6.1: 65–78.

Ramsey, Frank. 1990. "Truth and Probability." In *Frank Ramsey: Philosophical Papers*, ed. D. H. Mellor, 52–109. Cambridge, MA: Cambridge University Press.

Rohrschneider, Robert and Stephen Whitefield. 2009. "Understanding Cleavages in Party Systems: Issue Position and Issue Salience in 13 Post-Communist Democracies." *Comparative Political Studies* 42.2: 280–313.

Rosenfeld, Sam. 2017. *The Polarizers: Postwar Architects of Our Partisan Era*. Chicago: University of Chicago Press.

Rousseau, Jean-Jacques. 1988. *The Social Contract*. London: Penguin Classics.

Schkade, David, Cass R. Sunstein, and Daniel Kahneman. 2000. "Deliberating about Dollars: The Severity Shift." *Columbia Law Review* 100.4: 1139–1175.

Schmitt, Hermann and André Freire. 2012. "Ideological Polarisation: Different Worlds in East and West." In *Citizens and the European Polity: Mass Attitudes Towards the European and National Polities*, eds. David Sanders, Pedro Magalhaes, and Gabor Toka, 65–87. Oxford: Oxford University Press.

Schneider, Bill. 2018. *Standoff: How America Became Ungovernable*. New York: Simon and Schuster.

Schumpeter, Joseph A. 2008. *Capitalism, Socialism, and Democracy*. New York: HarperCollins Publishers.

Shah, Dhavan V., Douglas M. McLeod, Eunkyung Kim, Sun Young Lee, Melissa R. Gotlieb, Shirley S. Ho, and Hilde Breivik. 2007. "Political Consumerism: How Communication and Consumption Orientation Drive 'Lifestyle Politics'." *Annals of the American Academy of Political and Social Science* 611: 217–235.

Shi, Yongren, Kai Mast, Ingmar Weber, Agrippa Kellum, and Michael Macy. 2017. "Cultural Fault Lines and Political Polarization." *WebSci'17: Proceedings of the 2017 ACM on Web Sciences Conference*. https://ingmarweber.de/wp-content/uploads/2017/06/Cultural_Fault_Lines_and_Political_Polarization.pdf.

Sia, Choon-Ling, Bernard C. Y. Tan, and Kwok-Kee Wei. 2002. "Group Polarization and Computer-Mediated Communication: Effects of Communication: Cues, Social Presence, and Anonymity." *Information Systems Research* 13.1: 70–90.

Skocpol, Theda. 2013. *Diminished Democracy: From Membership to Management in American Civic Life*. Norman: University of Oklahoma Press.

Soh, Debra. 2018. "How to survive political disagreements with your family this holiday season," *Globe and Mail.* December 27. https://www.theglobeandmail.com/opinion/article-how-to-survive-political-disagreements-with-your-family-this-holiday/.

Somin, Ilya. 2016. *Democracy and Political Ignorance: Why Smaller Government Is Smarter.* Stanford, CA: Stanford University Press.

Stolle, Dietlind, and Michele Micheletti. 2013. *Political Consumerism: Global Responsibility in Action.* Cambridge, UK: Cambridge University Press.

Sunstein, Cass R. 2009. *Going to Extremes: How Like Minds Unite and Divide.* New York: Oxford University Press.

Sunstein, Cass R. 2015. *Choosing Not to Choose: Understanding the Value of Choice.* New York: Oxford University Press.

Sunstein, Cass R. 2017. *Republic: Divided Democracy in the Age of Social Media.* Princeton, NJ: Princeton University Press.

Tam Cho, Wendy K., James G. Gimpel, and Iris S. Hui. 2013. "Voter Migration and the Geographic Sorting of the American Electorate." *Annals of the Association of American Geographers* 103.4: 856–870.

Taylor, Paul. 2016a. "The demographic trends shaping 2016 and beyond." Pew Research Center. January 27. http://www.pewresearch.org/fact-tank/2016/01/27/the-demographic-trends-shaping-american-politics-in-2016-and-beyond/.

Taylor, Paul. 2016b. *The Next America: Boomers, Millennials, and the Looming Generational Showdown.* New York: Public Affairs.

Thaler, Richard H. and Cass R. Sunstein. 2003. "Libertarian Paternalism." *American Economic Review* 93.2: 175–179.

Thaler, Richard H. and Cass R. Sunstein. 2008. *Nudge: Improving Decisions About Health, Wealth, and Happiness.* New Haven, CT: Yale University Press.

Van Swol, Lyn M. 2009. "Extreme Members and Group Polarization." *Social Influence* 4.3: 185–199.

Vaidhyanathan, Siva. 2018. *Anti-Social Media: How Facebook Disconnects Us and Undermines Democracy.* New York: Oxford University Press.

Vinokur, Amiram and Eugene Burnstein. 1978. "Novel Argumentation and Attitude Change: The Case of Polarization Following Group Discussion." *European Journal of Social Psychology* 8.3: 335–348.

Wallace, R. Jay. 2013. *The View from Here: On Affirmation, Attachment, and the Limits of Regret.* New York: Oxford University Press.

Weber, Peter. 2013. "The politics of fast food: What Republicans and Democrats like to eat," *The Week.* February 27. http://theweek.com/articles/467272/politics-fast-food-what-republicans-democrats-like-eat.

Westfall, Jacob, Leaf Van Boven, John R. Chambers, and Charles M. Judd. 2015. "Perceiving Political Polarization in the United States: Party Identity Strength and Attitude Extremity Exacerbate the Perceived Partisan Divide." *Perspectives on Psychological Science* 10.2: 145–158.

Williamson, Thad. 2008. "Sprawl, Spatial Location, and Politics: How Ideological Identification Tracks the Built Environment." *American Politics Research* 36.6: 903–933.

Willingham, AJ. 2018. "How to talk politics at your family holiday dinner this year," *CNN.com*, November 22. https://www.cnn.com/2016/11/22/health/thanksgiving-holiday-conversation-survival-guide-trnd/index.html.

Wilson, Chris. 2014. "How Liberal Is Your Burger?" *Time*. November 10. http://time.com/3572348/republican-democrat-stores/.

Wilson, Reid. 2013. "You are where you shop: What your grocery store says about you," *Washington Post*. December 9. https://www.washingtonpost.com/blogs/govbeat/wp/2013/12/09/you-are-where-you-shop-what-your-grocery-store-says-about-you/?noredirect=on&utm_term=.a8f9a4937c13.

Wood, Thomas and Ethan Porter. 2019. "The Elusive Backfire Effect: Mass Attitudes' Steadfast Factual Adherence." *Political Behavior* 41.1: 135–163.

Young, Iris Marion. 1996. "Communication and the Other: Beyond Deliberative Democracy." In *Democracy and Difference: Contesting the Boundaries of the Political*, ed. Seyla Benhabib, 20–136. Princeton, NJ: Princeton University Press.

Zajonc, Robert. 1968. "Attitudinal Effects of Mere Exposure." *Journal of Personality and Social Psychology Monograph Supplement* 9.2: 1–27.

Index

For the benefit of digital users, indexed terms that span two pages (e.g., 52–53) may, on occasion, appear on only one of those pages.